BEATEN BY THE MASTERS

David Bird, known world-wide for his tales of the bridge-crazy monks of St Titus, moves to a hilarious new setting. Bridge is a compulsory subject at Cholmeley School and a host of vibrant characters participate in the action. Madame Baguette, the Senior French mistress, chases any master whose hair is still where it should be. They, meanwhile, turn a roving eye towards Yvonne Guitton, the nubile junior French mistress. And woe betide any unhappy boy (or member of staff) who finds himself partnering the irascible Headmaster.

As with all David Bird's books, it is not just a matter of the reader's being convulsed with laughter. The bridge is as brilliant as ever and by the time the final episode is reached, much sound bridge instruction has been painlessly absorbed. Which is more than can be said for those poor unfortunates, caught playing a torch-lit rubber after Lights Out.

Other humorous bridge fiction
in the Master Bridge Series

by David Bird
THE ABBOT AND THE SENSATIONAL SQUEEZE
ALL HANDS ON DECK!

by David Bird and Terence Reese
MIRACLES OF CARD PLAY
UNHOLY TRICKS
More Miraculous Card Play
DOUBLED AND VENERABLE
Further Miracles of Card Play
CARDINAL SINS
DIVINE INTERVENTION

by David Bird and Ron Klinger
KOSHER BRIDGE
KOSHER BRIDGE 2
THE RABBI'S MAGIC TRICK

by David Bird and Simon Cochemé
BACHELOR BRIDGE
BRIDGE WITH A FEMININE TOUCH

BEATEN BY
THE MASTERS

David Bird

CASSELL&CO
IN ASSOCIATION WITH
PETER CRAWLEY

First published in Great Britain 2001
in association with Peter Crawley
by Cassell & Co
Wellington House, 125 Strand, London WC2R 0BB
a member of the Orion Publishing Group

ISBN 0-304-35771-5

Typeset at The Spartan Press Ltd,
Lymington, Hants

Printed in Great Britain by
Mackays of Chatham, Kent

Contents

My warm thanks are due to friend and fellow writer, Tim Bourke of Australia, who gave me many of the best hands in this book.

1. The Headmaster's Self-Restraint

Bridge was a popular pastime at Cholmeley School and on this occasion the Prep Room had no fewer than fifteen tables in play. The participants were a varied mixture of pupils and staff, adolescent 13-year-olds competing with such as the decrepit 82-year-old Chaplain, the Reverend Benson.

The Headmaster, who was wearing his gown and mortarboard as always, gazed across the table at Benson. The cleric had been dummy on the previous hand and had nodded off at about trick seven. The old fool shouldn't still be teaching at his age, if truth be told. Still, with salaries the way they were in the 1960s, it would cost the earth to bring in some younger Chaplain to fill the post. Charles didn't seem to mind that he'd had no pay rise for two decades. Indeed, he was the only member of staff still to be paid in guineas.

'Move for the next round,' cried a voice from across the room.

The Headmaster nudged Reverend Benson into consciousness and assisted him towards Table 7, where two members of the sixth form awaited them. The Headmaster took his seat. First to speak, with the opponents vulnerable, he peered disapprovingly at this collection:

♠ K Q 8 6
♡ Q J
◇ Q J 3
♣ J 9 6 4

It was such an appalling hand, he could hardly believe it contained 12 points. One or two of the less experienced boys might venture a weak 1NT but no-one with any sense would consider it. The Headmaster removed the pipe from his mouth. 'No bid,' he said.

A few moments later the two sixth-formers had reached a slam. This was the full deal:

North–South game
Dealer West

```
                        ♠ A 7 5 4 2
                        ♡ A 5 3
                        ◇ 10 6
                        ♣ Q 8 7

        ♠ K Q 8 6          N          ♠ J 10 3
        ♡ Q J          W       E      ♡ 10 9 6
        ◇ Q J 3                        ◇ 9 8 7 5 2
        ♣ J 9 6 4          S          ♣ 10 3

                        ♠ 9
                        ♡ K 8 7 4 2
                        ◇ A K 4
                        ♣ A K 5 2
```

WEST	NORTH	EAST	SOUTH
Head-	James	Reverend	Stephen
Master	Dakin	Benson	Sutcliffe
Pass	1♠	Pass	2♡
Pass	3♡	Pass	4NT
Pass	5♡	Pass	6♡
End			

The Headmaster led ◇Q and stared in disbelief as the dummy was laid out. 'Did I hear the bidding correctly, Dakin?' he demanded. 'You made an opening bid on that hand?'

'Yes, Sir. All the top players open light nowadays,' replied James Dakin. 'The Americans, Kaplan and Kay, often open on ten or eleven points. I was reading about it last night, in *Bridge World*.'

'Kaplan and who?' exclaimed the Headmaster. 'You know perfectly well that dubious foreign magazines are not on the approved reading list. Bring them to my study tomorrow morning and I'll have them destroyed.'

The blond-haired Stephen Sutcliffe, who was school captain of both bridge and cricket, was no mean player for his age. He won the ◇Q lead with the ace and paused for thought. He would certainly need the trumps to be 3-2. Perhaps it would help if he set up a long spade.

Sutcliffe crossed to ♠A and ruffed a spade. Both defenders followed when the king and ace of trumps were played, and he ruffed another spade. A club to the queen permitted a third spade ruff, establishing a long card in the suit. Declarer then cashed one more high club, reaching this end position:

Dakin
♠ 7
♡ 5
♢ 10
♣ 8

Headmaster
♠ –
♡ –
♢ J 3
♣ J 9

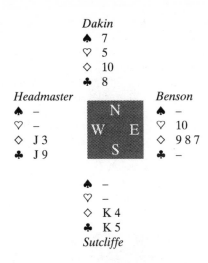

Benson
♠ –
♡ 10
♢ 9 8 7
♣ –

♠ –
♡ –
♢ K 4
♣ K 5

Sutcliffe

When ♣K was played, the Reverend Benson defended well by discarding a diamond. Had he ruffed instead, declarer would have been able to ruff one of his losers with ♡5, discarding the other loser on the long spade.

It was now Sutcliffe's chance to shine. If he continued carelessly with another club at this point, he would go down. East would overruff and there would be a further loser in diamonds. Stephen Sutcliffe made no such mistake. He cashed the diamond king and ruffed a diamond, claiming the contract. It was a strange hand. Although declarer had never made a trick with the long spade, the threat of doing so had allowed him to make the slam.

James Dakin opened the score-sheet. 'Good gracious!' he exclaimed. 'Several Easts have played in Two Diamonds doubled. It only went 500 down.'

'That's much less than the 1430 we made,' Sutcliffe observed.

Reverend Benson spread his cards face up on the baize. 'I don't see how I can overcall Two Diamonds on this collection,' he said. 'I only had one point.'

'Perhaps they opened 1NT on the Headmaster's hand?' suggested Sutcliffe. 'I would double on my 17-count and you would run to Two Diamonds.'

The ancient Chaplain looked across the table. 'Did you have an opening bid, Headmaster?' he enquired.

The Headmaster glared back at him. 'Had I been blessed with an opening bid, I would have opened,' he replied. 'Back in the 16th century our noble founder, Sir Roger Cholmeley, required a full fourteen points before opening. It's disgraceful how standards have slipped since those halcyon days.'

The next round saw the Headmaster facing the school Matron and Madame Baguette, the senior French mistress.

'Good evening, Headmaster,' said the Matron, a vague middle-aged woman who wore a nurse's uniform. 'Are you having your usual sparkling session?'

'Too many ludicrous results on the score-sheet tonight,' replied the Headmaster. 'I seem to perform at my best when the field is stronger.'

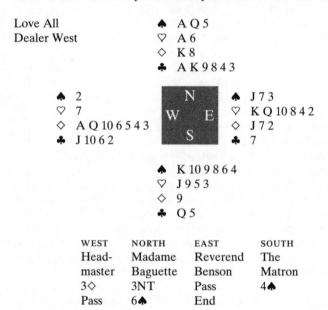

Love All
Dealer West

♠ A Q 5
♡ A 6
◇ K 8
♣ A K 9 8 4 3

♠ 2
♡ 7
◇ A Q 10 6 5 4 3
♣ J 10 6 2

♠ J 7 3
♡ K Q 10 8 4 2
◇ J 7 2
♣ 7

♠ K 10 9 8 6 4
♡ J 9 5 3
◇ 9
♣ Q 5

WEST	NORTH	EAST	SOUTH
Head-	Madame	Reverend	The
master	Baguette	Benson	Matron
3◇	3NT	Pass	4♠
Pass	6♠	End	

The Headmaster led ♡7 and down went the dummy. Matron assumed a thoughtful expression. She and Madame Baguette had not had the best of sessions, even by their own standards. How nice it would be if she could make some clever play against the Headmaster. 'Ace, please,' she said.

Matron drew trumps in three rounds, then turned to the club suit. She could not believe her bad luck when East showed out on the second round. A recent bridge column in *Children's Health Weekly* had claimed that a 3-2 break was more likely than not. She gave a small shake of the head. It just showed how you had to take what you read in those magazines with a pinch of salt. Now, how could she minimise the damage?

Matron threw one heart on ♣K, ruffed a club in her hand, then led a diamond towards the dummy. The Headmaster surveyed the scene with sinking spirits, chewing on the stem of his pipe. What had he done to deserve this? He rose with the ace of diamonds and had to play another diamond to dummy's king.

Matron threw another heart from her hand, then cast her eye on the two remaining clubs in dummy. Madame Baguette nodded encouragingly, hoping to indicate that the clubs were good.

'Try one of those clubs,' said the Matron. Hoping for the best, she threw the last loser from her hand. The club won the trick, she was pleased to see, and the slam had been made.

'It was difficult for you, Headmaster,' said the Matron, 'but if you happen to play another heart, I go down.'

'I didn't have another heart!' snapped the Headmaster. 'Of course I'd have played a heart if I had one.'

'It was your opening lead that caused the problem,' said the Reverend Benson. 'You needed to cash the ace of diamonds, then play a heart. Still, don't worry, Headmaster; *humanum est errare*.'

'I always lead an ace against a slam, myself,' the Matron observed. 'Then if partner has the king she can give you a come-on signal.'

A round or two later, the red-headed John Hutson caught his partner's eye. 'Look out!' he said. 'The Headmaster's coming our way.'

The Headmaster took his seat at the table and several moments later the ancient school Chaplain arrived. 'Sorry to keep you waiting,' said Reverend Benson. 'I thought Table 5 was over there, where Percy Cutforth is playing.'

The Headmaster gave a patient sigh. Table 5 had been by the stone fireplace for as long as he could remember. Ten years at least.

Reverend Benson settled in his chair. 'Now, me to bid, is it?' he said. 'Two spades.' This was a weak two, showing 6-10 points and a six-card suit.

John Hutson overcalled Four Hearts. The Headmaster passed and Neil Phillips, who had only recently taken up the game, bid Five Diamonds. Hutson's call of Six Hearts ended the auction and the Headmaster had to find a lead from this hand:

♠ 6
♡ 10 6 4
♢ A 8 6 2
♣ K 10 9 6 3

He turned imperiously to the red-headed declarer. 'What did your partner's Five Diamonds mean?' he demanded.

'I don't know, really,' Hutson replied. 'I thought it might be one of those, you know, cue-bids.'

'Oh dear,' said Neil Phillips. 'I didn't mean it as that.'

'You boys never know what you're doing,' declared the Headmaster, tossing his singleton spade on to the table . 'You're not allowed to play cue-bids until you're in the sixth form, anyway.'

This was the full deal:

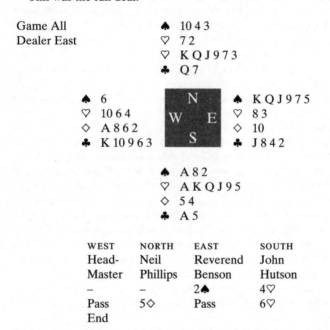

```
Game All                    ♠  10 4 3
Dealer East                 ♡  7 2
                            ♡  K Q J 9 7 3
                            ♣  Q 7

          ♠  6                          ♠  K Q J 9 7 5
          ♡  10 6 4                     ♡  8 3
          ◇  A 8 6 2                    ◇  10
          ♣  K 10 9 6 3                 ♣  J 8 4 2

                            ♠  A 8 2
                            ♡  A K Q J 9 5
                            ◇  5 4
                            ♣  A 5
```

WEST	NORTH	EAST	SOUTH
Head-	Neil	Reverend	John
Master	Phillips	Benson	Hutson
–	–	2♠	4♡
Pass	5◇	Pass	6♡
End			

John Hutson won the spade lead with the ace and drew trumps in three rounds. He then led a diamond from his hand. The Headmaster held up the ace and dummy's king won the trick, the 10 falling from East.

The young declarer gave a resigned nod. What a pity! If the Headmaster had taken the ace on the first round, he would have made the slam. He could then have thrown all his black-suit losers on dummy's diamond suit.

Hutson called for another high diamond from dummy and the Headmaster held up again, realising that he would be end-played if he won the trick. The young declarer looked somewhat mystified. He had escaped a diamond loser, for some reason, but he still had three black-suit losers. How about playing another high diamond? Yes, if the Headmaster made the mistake of holding up again, he could throw another black card and would go only two down.

A third round of diamonds was led and declarer threw a spade. The Headmaster drew deeply on his pipe, not liking the look of this at all. If he won with the diamond ace, he would have to give the lead to dummy, with a club or a diamond. Hoping that declarer would go wrong, he held up the ace of diamonds for the third time.

John Hutson could not believe his luck. The Headmaster was allowing him to dispose of one loser after another! 'Nine of diamonds, please,' he said.

The young declarer looked down at his hand. Should he throw a club or the last spade? It could hardly make any difference. Might as well throw the spade. The Headmaster had to admit defeat when this card appeared on the table. He won with $\diamondsuit A$ and exited with a club. Dummy's queen won the trick and the slam had been made.

Reverend Benson directed an annoyed glance across the table. The Headmaster had obviously not learnt his lesson from the earlier slam against the Matron. Had he led $\diamondsuit A$ and given him a diamond ruff, a club return would have put the slam three down! Even an initial club lead, allowing dummy's queen to make, would have put it two down.

Neil Phillips passed the travelling score-sheet to his partner. 'We're the only pair to bid it!' he exclaimed proudly. 'How would it go, playing cue-bids, Headmaster? Would we still have got there?'

The last round of the evening saw the arrival of Bertie Bellis, the popular Maths master, and Percy Cutforth, head of the Physics department. A more scientific partnership, it would be hard to imagine.

'Good evening, Headmaster,' said Bertie Bellis, taking his seat. 'You and Charles doing well?'

The Headmaster blew out a cloud of ill-smelling smoke. 'We haven't enjoyed the best of fortune,' he replied. 'Not that we can expect any sympathy from you two.'

The players drew their cards for this deal:

East–West game		♠ A 7 3	
Dealer South		♡ 2	
		◇ 8 7 5 2	
		♣ A K J 9 2	

♠ J 9 4			♠ Q 10 8 6 5
♡ A 10 8 7 6 3	N		♡ Q 9 5
◇ A 10	W E		◇ K 4
♣ 10 5	S		♣ 7 6 4

	♠ K 2
	♡ K J 4
	◇ Q J 9 6 3
	♣ Q 8 3

WEST	NORTH	EAST	SOUTH
Head-	Percy	Reverend	Bertie
master	Cutforth	Benson	Bellis
–	–	–	1NT
Pass	3NT	End	

The Headmaster led ♡7 against 3NT and down went the dummy. 'I hope you have a stopper in hearts, Bertie,' observed Percy Cutforth. 'Perhaps I should have bid it more slowly.'

The Reverend Benson produced the heart queen and Bellis won with the king. What now?

There were only eight top tricks and it seemed that he would have to play on the diamond suit. If West held ◇A K or ◇A K 4, all would be well. He would not be able to continue hearts from his side of the table without conceding a ninth trick.

Bertie Bellis crossed to ♣A and called for a diamond, the 4 appearing on his right. Spotting an extra chance, he played the 9 from his hand.

The Headmaster grabbed the trick with the 10 and paused to consider his continuation. East's ♡Q at trick one had marked declarer with the jack. It was long odds against this card now being bare. In any case, he could play for this chance when he won ◇A. For the moment, a spade switch must be right. If Charles held the king, that would serve as an entry for a heart lead through declarer's jack.

Bertie Bellis won the spade switch with dummy's ace, East playing an encouraging 8, and led another diamond. With a pained expression, the Headmaster had to overtake partner's king with the ace. He played another spade but Benson could produce only a disappointing queen. Bellis won with the king and claimed eleven tricks.

The Reverend Benson shook his head sadly. 'That wasn't very clever,' he observed. 'You should win the first diamond with the ace, Headmaster. Then I can take the second round with the king and play a heart through his stopper.'

'Don't be absurd!' snapped the Headmaster. 'How can I believe you have the king of diamonds? You should put up the king on the first round and fire a heart through. He goes three down, then.'

For a moment the Reverend Benson closed his eyes. It was typical of the Headmaster to blame partner for his own mistake. Minus 460 was bound to be a bottom.

'Clever move, that ♢9, Bertie,' said Percy Cutforth, chuckling to himself. 'If you play the queen, you force the Headmaster to get it right.'

The Headmaster glared to his left. Was Cutforth aware that the pay-rise calculations were being made next week?

'Perhaps you should cash the ace of hearts, Headmaster,' suggested Benson. 'At least that would hold it to 430.'

'You gave me an encouraging eight of spades,' retorted the Head-master. 'I naturally assumed you held the spade king.'

Benson gave a sigh. Was it his fault he had been dealt the queen of spades instead of the king? It was a singularly thankless task, partnering the Headmaster. Still, maybe all this suffering, so nobly borne, would bring its reward one day – in the not too distant future, when he approached the Pearly Gates.

The Headmaster was already sorting his cards for the next deal. 'Rise with the diamond king,' he declared again. 'That was the answer.'

The Reverend Benson gave a pious nod of the head. 'Sorry, Headmaster,' he said.

2. The Founder's Salver

Once a year six masters and six boys contested an individual tournament for the Founder's Salver. Donated by the widow of some undistinguished old boy, the salver was solid silver and bore the crest of the school's founder, Sir Roger Cholmeley.

The first round saw the Headmaster at a table with Stephen Sutcliffe, Madame Baguette, and John Hutson.

East–West game
Dealer North

```
                    ♠ K 10
                    ♡ K 5
                    ◇ A K 6 4 2
                    ♣ 10 8 6 3
     ♠ 6 5              N          ♠ Q 7 4 2
     ♡ Q J 8 2      W     E        ♡ 9 3
     ◇ J 9 7 5                     ◇ Q 10 3
     ♣ K 7 2            S          ♣ A Q J 5
                    ♠ A J 9 8 3
                    ♡ A 10 7 6 4
                    ◇ 8
                    ♣ 9 4
```

WEST	NORTH	EAST	SOUTH
Madame	John	Stephen	Head-
Baguette	Hutson	Sutcliffe	master
–	1◇	Pass	1♠
Pass	1NT	Pass	4♡
Pass	4♠	End	

'The 1NT rebid?' queried Madame Baguette, who was on lead.

'We're playing a weak no-trump,' the Headmaster replied, 'so the 1NT rebid shows 15-17.'

Madame Baguette led ♣2 and down went the dummy. 'I thought you played the 1NT rebid as wide-range,' apologised Hutson. 'I meant to show 12-16 points. Sorry, Sir.'

'I've never heard of such an absurd idea,' muttered the Headmaster. 'With a 12-14 hand you would have opened 1NT, wouldn't you?'

The defenders persisted with clubs and the Headmaster ruffed the third round with the 3. Everyone followed to the two top hearts and Madame Baguette played a mildly deceptive queen on the third round. 'Ruff with the king,' said the Headmaster.

The precaution proved worthwhile. Had he ruffed low, East would have overruffed and returned another trump, defeating the contract. The Headmaster continued with the ace and king of diamonds, throwing a heart. He then ruffed a diamond with the ace, again protecting himself from an overruff and a trump continuation.

The Headmaster ruffed his last heart with the 10 and faced his remaining cards, claiming the contract. 'You can score the queen of trumps when you like,' he said.

'Oh, well done, Sir!' exclaimed Hutson. 'Excellent safety play.'

The Headmaster nodded. 'You're lucky you were playing with me when the deal arose,' he replied.

The first change of partnerships placed the Headmaster opposite Madame Baguette.

Game All
Dealer West

	♠	8 7 4
	♡	A Q 3
	◇	A 10
	♣	A K Q 7 6

♠	A Q J 9 2			♠	6 3
♡	J 9 8 7 6	N		♡	5
◇	K Q	W E		◇	J 9 8 7 2
♣	2	S		♣	J 10 9 5 4

	♠	K 10 5
	♡	K 10 4 2
	◇	6 5 4 3
	♣	8 3

WEST	NORTH	EAST	SOUTH
Head-	John	Madame	Stephen
master	Hutson	Baguette	Sutcliffe
1♠	Dble	Pass	1NT
Pass	3NT	End	

The Headmaster rated all four of his suits equally unattractive, as far as the opening lead was concerned. Eventually he tried his luck with the singleton club. Sutcliffe won with dummy's ace and cashed two more rounds of the suit, throwing a diamond from the South hand. The Headmaster threw one heart and one spade.

When Sutcliffe played the ace and queen of hearts, East showed out on the second round, marking the Headmaster with 5-5-2-1 shape. Sutcliffe continued with ace and another diamond, throwing West on lead. This was the position:

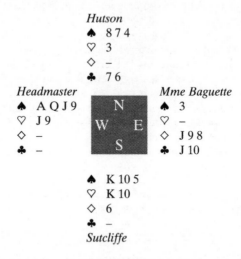

Hutson
♠ 8 7 4
♡ 3
◇ –
♣ 7 6

Headmaster
♠ A Q J 9
♡ J 9
◇ –
♣ –

Mme Baguette
♠ 3
♡ –
◇ J 9 8
♣ J 10

Sutcliffe
♠ K 10 5
♡ K 10
◇ 6
♣ –

The Headmaster could see that he would have to concede one trick. His concern was to avoid a second endplay, which would give declarer the contract. If he played the ace and queen of spades he would surely be thrown back in with a spade, forced to lead into the heart tenace. The Headmaster therefore tried the effect of a heart exit.

Sutcliffe gratefully accepted the two heart tricks and then exited with ♠10. His luck was in. The Headmaster had to win and concede a trick to declarer's ♠K. The game had been made.

Aware that any gloating would be out of place, John Hutson restricted himself to a quiet 'Well played, partner.'

Madame Baguette was less restrained. 'Could you not see this coming, Headmaster?' she said. 'If you throw king-queen of diamonds on the clubs, he cannot do it. I have good diamonds here.'

The Headmaster was unaccustomed to having his play criticised, particularly by some foreign woman in front of two boys. 'A facile analysis, Madame Baguette,' he declared. 'If I throw a diamond honour on the second club, declarer won't cash the third club. He will endplay me with a low diamond immediately.'

Partnerships were now changed for the second time.

North–South game
Dealer West

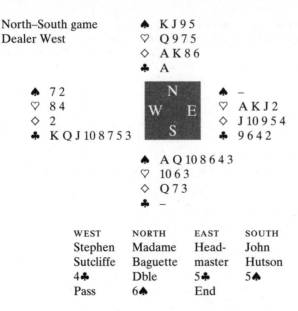

<pre>
♠ K J 9 5
♡ Q 9 7 5
◇ A K 8 6
♣ A
</pre>

<pre>
♠ 7 2
♡ 8 4
◇ 2
♣ K Q J 10 8 7 5 3
</pre>

<pre>
♠ –
♡ A K J 2
◇ J 10 9 5 4
♣ 9 6 4 2
</pre>

<pre>
♠ A Q 10 8 6 4 3
♡ 10 6 3
◇ Q 7 3
♣ –
</pre>

WEST	NORTH	EAST	SOUTH
Stephen	Madame	Head-	John
Sutcliffe	Baguette	master	Hutson
4♣	Dble	5♣	5♠
Pass	6♠	End	

Stephen Sutcliffe led his singleton diamond against the spade slam. The Headmaster looked anxiously at the dummy. It was annoying not to have received a heart lead. However, unless declarer had an 8-card spade suit, it seemed that he would not have twelve tricks at his disposal.

Hutson won the diamond lead with the ace and cashed ♣A, throwing a heart. He then ran the trumps, arriving at this position:

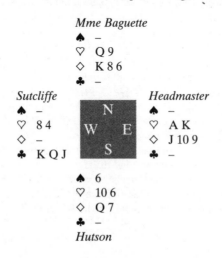

Mme Baguette
<pre>
♠ –
♡ Q 9
◇ K 8 6
♣ –
</pre>

Sutcliffe
<pre>
♠ –
♡ 8 4
◇ –
♣ K Q J
</pre>

Headmaster
<pre>
♠ –
♡ A K
◇ J 10 9
♣ –
</pre>

Hutson
<pre>
♠ 6
♡ 10 6
◇ Q 7
♣ –
</pre>

Hutson led the last trump, throwing $\heartsuit$9 from dummy. The Headmaster now had one further discard to make. The opening diamond lead had clearly been a singleton, so he could not afford to release his guard in that suit. His only chance was to throw a heart honour, in the hope that his partner held $\heartsuit$10.

When $\heartsuit$K appeared on the table, Hutson played a heart to the queen and ace. His $\heartsuit$10 was good for a twelfth trick and, as a result of winning the opening lead in the dummy, the diamond queen would serve as an entry.

'Such a nice play, he makes there!' exclaimed Madame Baguette. She turned towards the Headmaster. 'If only his French composition was so good.'

The Headmaster could not care less about Hutson's foreign language capabilities. He glared across the table. 'Can't you lead a heart?' he demanded. 'I would score three tricks in the suit.'

The half-time score-sheet showed these players in the lead:

1st Headmaster	*61.7%*
2nd Sutcliffe	*58.8%*
3rd Mr Bellis	*57.1%*
4th Mr Cutforth	*56.3%*
5th Paulson	*52.6%*
6th Mr Butcher	*51.1%*

'I can't believe those scores,' said Simon Paulson. 'Bertie Bellis is only third. I thought he would win by a mile.'

'Are you forgetting something?' demanded a deep voice.

Paulson spun round to find the Headmaster standing just behind him.

'Mr Bellis plays all his bridge with a very strong partner, Mr Cutforth,' continued the Headmaster. 'Certain other players, whom you may underestimate, have less able partners.'

Paulson swallowed hard. 'Good point, Sir,' he replied.

The second half started and the Headmaster continued to fare well. The last round saw him at a table with the Reverend Benson, Neil Phillips and Simon Paulson.

'I'm miles below average now,' said Neil Phillips. 'I doubled Mr Bellis into game on the last round.'

The Headmaster grimaced. Typical of these boys to mess around when they were out of contention. Didn't they realise they were affecting the relative standing of the experts in the field?

'You should try your best right until the end, Phillips,' he reprimanded. 'It's unfair to the other contestants otherwise.'

'I *was* trying my best, Sir,' Phillips replied. 'Mr Bellis was vulnerable and I read in some bridge book that plus 200 was always a good pairs score. The Golden 200, they called it.'

'And what did this worthy tome have to say about the Golden Minus 670?' continued the Headmaster. 'Did it commend that too?'

This was the first board of the round:

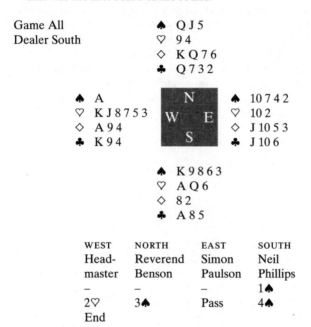

Game All   ♠ Q J 5
Dealer South   ♡ 9 4
                 ♢ K Q 7 6
                 ♣ Q 7 3 2

♠ A   ♠ 10 7 4 2
♡ K J 8 7 5 3   ♡ 10 2
♢ A 9 4   ♢ J 10 5 3
♣ K 9 4   ♣ J 10 6

         ♠ K 9 8 6 3
         ♡ A Q 6
         ♢ 8 2
         ♣ A 8 5

WEST	NORTH	EAST	SOUTH
Head-	Reverend	Simon	Neil
master	Benson	Paulson	Phillips
–	–	–	1♠
2♡	3♠	Pass	4♠
End			

Anxious to avoid being endplayed, the Headmaster led the ace of trumps. 'Good gracious, Charles!' he exclaimed, when the dummy went down. 'You don't have much there for a double raise.'

'*Audere est facere*,' observed the Reverend Benson. 'In any case, it's important to show faith in the boys' cardplay.'

The Headmaster continued with ace and another diamond, dummy's king winning the trick. Phillips drew two more rounds of trumps with the queen and jack, then discarded a heart on ♢Q. He reached his hand with a diamond ruff, drew the last trump, and led a small club towards dummy.

The Headmaster paused to consider his defence. If declarer held three clubs to the ace, which was likely, going in with the king would allow him to score three club tricks. The Headmaster eventually played low on the first round of clubs, dummy's queen winning the trick. Phillips returned to his hand with the club ace and played a third round of the suit, won by West's king. For a second the Headmaster closed his eyes. What was the matter with him? Why hadn't he unblocked the king under the ace? His partner could then have won the third round with the jack.

The Headmaster played a heart, hoping for a miracle, but no divine intervention was forthcoming. Neil Phillips won the last two tricks with his heart tenace and the game had been made.

'Good effort, Phillips!' exclaimed Reverend Benson. 'You certainly caught the Headmaster sleeping there.'

Phillips smiled nervously. 'I was bearing in mind what the Headmaster said,' he replied. 'That we should all try our best.'

A few moments later, the Headmaster and Phillips found themselves in partnership.

East–West game
Dealer South

```
                      ♠ J 10 3
                      ♡ J 10 2
                      ◇ K Q J 7 5
                      ♣ A 2
    ♠ 8 4            N            ♠ 9 7 5
    ♡ Q 7 3      W       E        ♡ 9 6
    ◇ A 10 3 2                    ◇ 8 6 4
    ♣ K 10 5 3       S            ♣ J 8 7 6 4
                      ♠ A K Q 6 2
                      ♡ A K 8 5 4
                      ◇ 9
                      ♣ Q 9
```

WEST	NORTH	EAST	SOUTH
Head-	Simon	Neil	Reverend
master	Paulson	Phillips	Benson
–	–	–	1♠
Pass	2◇	Pass	2♡
Pass	4♠	Pass	4NT
Pass	5◇	Pass	6♠
End			

The Headmaster surveyed his hand uncertainly. A club lead might work but it was risky. Perhaps a trump would be wiser.

The Reverend Benson won the trump lead with the queen and immediately led his singleton diamond. The Headmaster did not like the look of things. If Benson held the queen of clubs, a club lead would have beaten the slam. Anyway, it was surely hopeless to rise with the diamond ace. Declarer would make four diamond tricks.

Dummy's ◇K won the trick and Benson ruffed a diamond. His next move was to lead a low heart towards dummy. The Headmaster rose with the queen and returned another trump, won by dummy's jack. A second diamond ruff with the ace was followed by a heart to the 10 and a third diamond ruff, bringing down the Headmaster's ◇A. Benson re-entered dummy with ♣A and drew East's last trump with the 10. He then threw the club queen on the established diamond and claimed the contract.

The elderly cleric smiled happily at his young partner. 'I think that was the best line,' he declared. 'I didn't want to let you down.'

The Headmaster reached resignedly for his score-card. Why were his opponents suddenly playing like world champions?

For the last board of the event, the Headmaster would have his regular partner opposite him. He stole a quick glance at the ancient cleric. Exhausted by his efforts on the last hand, his eyes were half-closed. Surely he wouldn't choose this particular moment to fall asleep, thought the Headmaster. Didn't he realise that his partner still had an excellent chance of winning the event?

North–South game
Dealer South

```
                    ♠ 8 6 5
                    ♡ 9 7 4 2
                    ◇ K 7 3
                    ♣ 7 4 3

    ♠ 10 7 2              N          ♠ K Q 9 4 3
    ♡ A K Q 5       W         E      ♡ J 10 6 3
    ◇ 9 5                S           ◇ J 10 8 4
    ♣ 10 9 6 5                       ♣ —

                    ♠ A J
                    ♡ 8
                    ◇ A Q 6 2
                    ♣ A K Q J 8 2
```

WEST	NORTH	EAST	SOUTH
Neil	Reverend	Simon	Head-
Phillips	Benson	Paulson	master
–	–	–	2♣
2♡	Pass	4♡	5♣
End			

West began the defence with two top hearts. The Headmaster ruffed the second round and drew the outstanding trumps, noting that West held all four of them. East, meanwhile, had been finding difficulty with his discards. He threw two spades, followed by the ♡J and 10.

It was clear to the Headmaster that East had the diamond suit guarded. In that case, the only possible chance was to find him with the king-queen of spades and to effect a squeeze. But how could the count be rectified?

The Headmaster soon spotted the answer to his problem. The squeeze would take place at the same moment he rectified the count! He played his last trump, East throwing another spade, then crossed to ◇K. This was the end position:

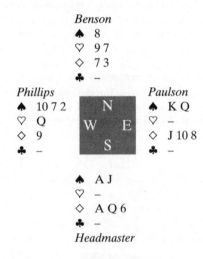

<pre>
                    Benson
                    ♠ 8
                    ♡ 9 7
                    ◇ 7 3
                    ♣ —
    Phillips   Paulson
    ♠ 10 7 2   N   ♠ K Q
    ♡ Q   W   E   ♡ —
    ◇ 9   ◇ J 10 8
    ♣ —   S   ♣ —
                    ♠ A J
                    ♡ —
                    ◇ A Q 6
                    ♣ —
                    Headmaster
</pre>

'Nine of hearts, please,' said the Headmaster.

Simon Paulson froze in his seat, uncertain which card to throw. Eventually he discarded ♠Q, hoping that his partner held the jack of the suit. The Headmaster threw ◇6 from his hand and West won with the heart queen. 'The rest are mine,' declared the Headmaster, fanning his remaining four cards on the table.

The two fourth-formers exchanged a glance. Was there anything they could have done about it?

The Headmaster reached for a large white handkerchief and proceeded to mop his brow. 'A losing-card squeeze, if I'm not mistaken', he said. 'We can count ourselves extremely lucky to have witnessed such a hand!'

3. The New Art Master

Phillip Glasson, the new art master, had attracted a good deal of attention among the female members of staff. There was no shortage of male teachers, of course, but most of them were well past their sell-by-date. Kathy Parker, the gym mistress, claimed that Glasson had more hair on his head than the rest of the male staff put together. An exaggeration, of course, but not much of one.

The Matron spotted Glasson approaching down the corridor and reached inside her handbag, proceeding to check her appearance in a small mirror. Yes, that Hot Strawberry lipstick made her look ten years younger. She must be in with a chance.

'Hello, Phillip,' said the Matron. 'I've been let down by my partner for next Wednesday. I was wondering if you and I might have a session together.'

'Nothing would please me more, Matron,' Glasson replied.

The Matron felt a tingle flowing through her. Yes! It had been three-and-sixpence well invested. Such an enticing shade of red.

'Unfortunately I've already agreed to play with Yvonne Goutier,' Glasson continued. 'She's only a beginner at the game but we enjoy playing together.'

The Matron sucked in her cheeks. He was partnering the junior French mistress *again*? What on earth could he see in such a thin girl? There wasn't an ounce of flesh on her; she should see a doctor. The Matron summoned her best smile. 'Some other time, perhaps?' she said.

Glasson gave a non-committal nod and continued on his way down the corridor.

The following Wednesday the Matron was back in harness with Madame Baguette, the senior French mistress. It was with mixed feelings that she saw Phillip Glasson approaching their table, his skimpily-clad partner in tow.

'Ah, good, you did manage to find a partner, Matron,' said Glasson, taking his seat.

Madame Baguette looked puzzled. Find a partner? Did not she and the Matron always play together?

This was the first board of the round:

```
Love All            ♠  A Q 4
Dealer East         ♡  K 7 5 2
                    ◇  J 2
                    ♣  A K 7 5

    ♠  J 6 3          N          ♠  10 9 8 5
    ♡  10 9      W         E     ♡  A 8 6 3
    ◇  Q 9 8 4                   ◇  7 6 3
    ♣  10 8 6 3       S          ♣  9 2

                    ♠  K 7 2
                    ♡  Q J 4
                    ◇  A K 10 5
                    ♣  Q J 4
```

WEST	NORTH	EAST	SOUTH
The	Yvonne	Madame	Phillip
Matron	Goutier	Baguette	Glasson
–	–	Pass	1NT
Pass	6NT	End	

'Weak no-trump, is it?' said the Matron, who was on lead.

Yvonne Goutier turned her almond eyes towards the handsome declarer. 'No, no, Phillip is 'elping me by playing the French methods,' she replied. 'It is best for Phillip and I to do that. I 'ave not learnt the Acol yet.'

Madame Baguette winced. 'For Phillip and *me* to do that,' she said sternly. 'Accusative case after a preposition.'

'It's not a weak no-trump, then?' persisted the Matron.

'No, Phillip and me play strong no-trump.'

Madame Baguette gave up the struggle. No-one under thirty had the faintest idea about grammar nowadays. Not even schoolteachers. 'You to lead, Matron,' she said.

The Matron was an avid reader of the bridge column in *Children's Health Weekly*. Recently she had read that you should always look for a safe lead against 6NT. What should it be, a heart or a club? A heart looked safer, with those two touching cards.

Unwilling to give declarer three heart tricks, Madame Baguette held off her ace. Glasson won with the jack and crossed to dummy with a spade. When a second round of hearts was led, Madame Baguette was again reluctant to play her ace. Indeed, had she done so, declarer would have had twelve tricks.

Glasson won with the heart queen and the 9 fell from West. Now, how did the hearts lie? If they were 3-3, a third round of the suit would establish a twelfth trick. If the lead had been from 10 9 doubleton, he would need to take a diamond finesse instead. Which line should he take? To play on hearts would rely on just one chance – that the hearts were 3-3. To finesse in diamonds would give him two chances: the finesse might succeed, or it might fail but West would then have no heart to return.

Phillip Glasson returned to dummy with a spade and ran the jack of diamonds. The finesse lost but when a club was returned Glasson was able to claim twelve tricks.

'You had no heart to play?' Madame Baguette exclaimed.

'I'm afraid not,' replied the Matron. 'You should have taken your ace of hearts before he played on diamonds.'

'No, you were quite right not to take the heart ace,' said Glasson, returning his hands to the wallet. 'You ladies defended very well. You made it difficult for me.'

Yvonne Goutier inspected the score-sheet. 'Most tables 'ave the same result,' she announced.

'I expect the other Wests made it easy by leading a diamond from Matron's hand,' said Glasson. 'Quite wrong against 6NT. You should look for a safe lead, as Matron did here.'

The Matron sat back in her chair, a contented expression on her face. Had she been thirty years younger, things would have been different. Very different. It was obvious that Glasson fancied her but he was deterred by modern-day prejudice against an age gap. Never mind, perhaps she would have another pleasant dream about him tonight. A small smile came to her lips. The one last night had been particularly good.

Glasson turned towards Madame Baguette. 'You must find Yvonne, here, a very welcome addition to the French department,' he declared. 'She's a promising bridge player, too.'

Madame Baguette glared disapprovingly at her underling. What bad taste to wear such a flimsy dress in front of the boys. As for her being a promising player . . . she had never heard such nonsense! The girl could hardly tell one card from another.

The players drew their cards for the second board of the round.

East–West game
Dealer South

```
                    ♠  A 7 2
                    ♡  8 5
                    ◇  A 10 6 2
                    ♣  A Q 8 3

    ♠  10 9 4              N              ♠  K J 6 5
    ♡  A Q J 9 4      W         E         ♡  10 6
    ◇  Q J 5                              ◇  9 7 3
    ♣  7 2                S               ♣  10 9 6 5

                    ♠  Q 8 3
                    ♡  K 7 3 2
                    ◇  K 8 4
                    ♣  K J 4
```

WEST	NORTH	EAST	SOUTH
The	Yvonne	Madame	Phillip
Matron	Goutier	Baguette	Glasson
–	–	–	1♣
1♡	3♣	Pass	3NT
End			

Glasson was playing a strong no-trump, to accommodate his partner, and therefore had to open a Prepared Club. When the Matron overcalled in hearts, Yvonne Goutier surveyed her cards uncertainly. The ♡8 5 was not a reliable stopper, so bidding in no-trumps would be *dangéreux*. She could raise the partner's clubs, but surely she was too powerful for bidding just 2♣. 'Three Clubs,' she said.

Phillip Glasson could sense a good hand opposite. He bid 3NT, ending the bidding, and the Matron now had to find a lead. Unwilling to concede a trick to declarer's presumed king of hearts, she tried her luck with ♠10. Madame Baguette won with the king and switched to ♡10. Glasson played low and ducked again when hearts were continued. The Matron won with the 9 and paused to assess the situation. Was declarer's ♡K bare now? No, Madame Baguette was re-arranging her hand and must therefore be out of hearts. A safe spade exit seemed best.

Glasson won West's spade return in the dummy and cashed four rounds of clubs, throwing a diamond from his hand. These cards remained:

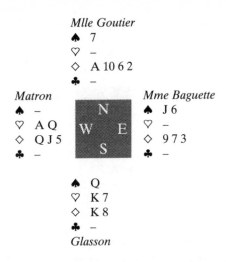

Mlle Goutier
♠ 7
♡ –
♦ A 10 6 2
♣ –

Matron
♠ –
♡ A Q
♦ Q J 5
♣ –

Mme Baguette
♠ J 6
♡ –
♦ 9 7 3
♣ –

♠ Q
♡ K 7
♦ K 8
♣ –
Glasson

When a spade was played to the queen, the Matron did not like the situation at all. If she threw a diamond, declarer would surely have four diamond tricks. Reluctantly, she discarded ♡Q. Glasson now exited with ♡7, setting up the heart king as his ninth trick.

Yvonne Goutier beamed across the table. 'I was not sure what to bid,' she said. 'I am so glad my bid of 3♣ has finished well.'

'Your 3♣ response was absurd,' declared Madame Baguette. 'You had 14 points facing an opening bid.'

'I was sure Phillip would make another move,' the French girl replied.

Madame Baguette turned her eyes to a different target. 'You must lead a low heart, Matron,' she declared. 'My 10 forces the king and Phillip has no chance.'

'Is that right?' queried Glasson. 'I can cash four rounds of clubs and Matron has to throw two spades. Then I cash the spade ace and endplay her with a heart. She would have to give me three diamond tricks.'

The Matron gave the art master a grateful pat on the shoulder. My word, what muscles he had! She hadn't felt anything like that since the War. 'Quite right, young man,' she said. 'That's exactly the conclusion I came to.'

This was the last board of the round:

Game All   ♠ Q 10 4
Dealer North   ♡ A Q 10 9 3
                ◇ 10 7
                ♣ K J 5

```
      ♠ K 3              N        ♠ 8 7 6 5 2
      ♡ K 7 6 2     W         E   ♡ 8 5
      ◇ K Q J 3                   ◇ A 9 6
      ♣ 9 7 3             S       ♣ 8 6 2
```

              ♠ A J 9
              ♡ J 4
              ◇ 8 5 4 2
              ♣ A Q 10 4

WEST	NORTH	EAST	SOUTH
The	Yvonne	Madame	Phillip
Matron	Goutier	Baguette	Glasson
–	1♡	Pass	2♣
Pass	3♣	Pass	3NT
End			

Glasson ended in 3NT and the Matron led the king of diamonds.
Madame Baguette nodded her approval, backing this up with an
encouraging ◇9. The Matron continued with a low diamond to her
partner's ace and the defenders soon had four diamond tricks in the
bag.

The Matron surveyed her remaining cards. What now? She could
hardly lead a heart from the king, with the ace-queen sitting over her.
A spade was risky too, since declarer was likely to hold the ace. Ah
well, it would have to be a club.

Glasson won the ♣9 switch with dummy's king. Since a successful
spade finesse would bring in only eight tricks, he saw he would have to
play on hearts. He crossed to ♣10 and led ♡J. The Matron detached
the king for a moment, then looked closely at dummy's hearts. On
second thoughts, there wasn't much point in covering. Dummy's hearts
would then all be good. She replaced the king with the 2 and Glasson
ran the jack successfully.

Before repeating the heart finesse, Glasson decided to cash two
more club tricks. This was the position when he led the fourth round of
clubs:

Mlle Goutier
♠ Q 10
♡ A Q 10
◇ –
♣ –

Matron
♠ K 3
♡ K 7 6
◇ –
♣ –

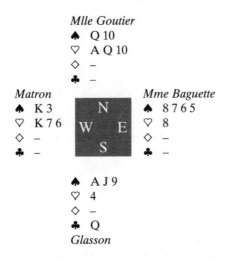

Mme Baguette
♠ 8 7 6 5
♡ 8
◇ –
♣ –

♠ A J 9
♡ 4
◇ –
♣ Q
Glasson

Matron paused to consider her discard on ♣Q. A spade was out of the question, surely, since the ace would then drop her king. When she eventually threw ♡6, Glasson repeated the heart finesse. The ace then dropped West's king and the game had been made.

Madame Baguette was far from overjoyed at suffering a third consecutive bottom against her young compatriot. 'Throw a spade, partner, and he goes down,' she exclaimed. 'When the heart king does not fall, he will take a spade finesse.'

The Matron gazed blankly across the table. Throw a spade? Wouldn't her king fall, then?

Phillip Glasson turned towards Madame Baguette. 'I was wondering if you could beat it by switching to a spade at Trick 3,' he said.

The Matron nodded emphatically. 'Yes, that would set up five tricks for us,' she said. 'Four diamonds and a spade.'

Madame Baguette glared at the Art Master. This was the famous British chivalry? To point out a mistake made by a lady?

'But, of course, I would simply win with the ace of spades and cash four club tricks,' Glasson continued. 'The last club would catch Matron in a strip squeeze. If she holds all her winners and throws a heart, I can bring in the heart suit. If she throws a winner, I can set up a ninth trick in spades.'

Madame Baguette sent an admiring glance in Glasson's direction. What a card-player the man was. And in her experience men who were good at one thing were generally good at another. He would soon tire of that hopeless stick insect and then . . . *sacré bleu*, what fun the two of them would have together!

4. Rupert Broke's Initiation Rites

At Cholmeley School no boy's education was considered complete until he had played a session in partnership with the Headmaster. It went without saying that this was a frightening experience, comparable to the circumcision rites in certain parts of Africa.

'So, it's the great night, tonight, is it?' said Luke Davison, giving his colleague a friendly nudge.

'You wouldn't joke about it if it was your turn,' replied the 15-year-old Rupert Broke. 'Remember what happened to Smithers minor last term?'

The first round of the Pairs pitted the new partnership against Bertie Bellis. The Maths master had little interest in bidding but was regarded, in school terms at any rate, as a top-class card player. This was the first board of the round:

```
Love All                    ♠ 8 6 4 2
Dealer East                 ♡ 10
                            ◇ K 6 4 3
                            ♣ K 8 5 2

        ♠ Q 7          N          ♠ A K J 10 9 3
        ♡ 9 4 3 2                 ♡ 5
        ◇ Q J 7 5   W     E       ◇ 10 9 2
        ♣ Q 10 4       S          ♣ J 7 3

                            ♠ 5
                            ♡ A K Q J 8 7 6
                            ◇ A 8
                            ♣ A 9 6
```

WEST	NORTH	EAST	SOUTH
Head-	Reverend	Rupert	Bertie
master	Benson	Broke	Bellis
–	–	2♠	Dble
Pass	3♣	Pass	4♡
Pass	5♡	Pass	6♡
End			

The Headmaster led ♠Q and down went the dummy. 'I don't know if you agree with my 5♡ bid,' Benson observed. 'You bid game on your own hand, though, and I might have had nothing.'

'Good bid, Charles,' Bellis replied. 'The two kings are good cards.'

Rupert Broke overtook the spade lead with his king and attempted to cash the ace of spades. Bellis ruffed in the South hand, crossed to ♡10, and ruffed a spade with the ace. He then drew trumps in three more rounds.

Most of the players in the room would have seen little prospect of making the slam. Bellis could see a route to twelve tricks, provided West had started with at least four diamonds. He cashed ♢A, crossed to ♢K, and ruffed a diamond. These cards remained:

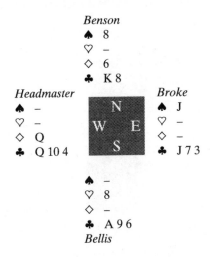

```
                    Benson
                    ♠  8
                    ♡  –
                    ♢  6
                    ♣  K 8
   Headmaster                      Broke
   ♠  –              N             ♠  J
   ♡  –          W       E         ♡  –
   ♢  Q                            ♢  –
   ♣  Q 10 4          S            ♣  J 7 3
                    ♠  –
                    ♡  8
                    ♢  –
                    ♣  A 9 6
                    Bellis
```

When the last trump was led the Headmaster discarded a club, retaining his guard on dummy's last diamond. Bellis threw dummy's ♢6, which had performed its role nobly, and young Rupert Broke was now pressed for a discard. Since it would clearly give away a trick to throw ♠J, he too decided to discard a club. Bellis proceeded to score three club tricks, making the slam.

The Headmaster looked uncertainly towards Bertie Bellis. 'You needed both club honours intact for that ending, didn't you?' he said.

'I think so,' Bellis replied.

The Headmaster glared blackly at his young partner. 'Switch to a club at Trick 2, boy!' he exclaimed. 'That breaks up the squeeze.'

Rupert Broke blinked nervously. 'Sorry, Headmaster,' he said. 'I er . . . did think about it.'

'You thought about it and still got it wrong?' thundered the Headmaster. 'Leave me on lead at Trick 1, in that case. A club switch would be automatic for a player of my calibre. What on earth was the point of overtaking? Mr Bellis wouldn't bid a slam with two top losers, would he?'

'I'm very sorry, Sir.'

The Headmaster patted his pockets, searching for his pipe. 'You certainly will be if you continue to play so carelessly,' he said.

Reverend Benson unfolded the score-sheet and entered the 980 in his usual shaky handwriting. 'Some of the boys will pass Four Hearts on my hand,' he said. 'Perhaps when they get to my age they'll appreciate the value of two kings.'

A few moments later Bertie Bellis was in another slam.

North–South game
Dealer West

```
                        ♠ A 6 5
                        ♡ J 5 4 2
                        ◇ 7 5
                        ♣ A 9 6 3
     ♠ 8 3                              ♠ 10 4
     ♡ 10 9 7              N            ♡ Q 8 6 3
     ◇ K Q 9 8 6 4 3 2   W   E          ◇ —
     ♣ —                   S            ♣ Q J 10 8 7 4 2
                        ♠ K Q J 9 7 2
                        ♡ A K
                        ◇ A J 10
                        ♣ K 5
```

WEST	NORTH	EAST	SOUTH
Head-master	Reverend Benson	Rupert Broke	Bertie Bellis
4◇	Pass	Pass	Dble
Pass	4♡	Pass	4♠
Pass	6♠	Pass	6NT
End			

The Headmaster led ♡10 and an amused Reverend Benson laid out the dummy. 'If it was right to give you a single raise with two kings,' he said, 'it must be right to bid a slam with two aces.'

'Quite so,' Bertie Bellis replied. 'You bid it well.'

Unfortunately, thought Bellis, it seemed that he had not bid it too well himself. In Six Spades he could doubtless have led towards the ace of diamonds and manoeuvred a diamond ruff with the ace. What were the prospects in 6NT? If West had led from four hearts, it would be possible to duck out East's ♡Q, setting up the jack. That wasn't very likely. A better chance was to aim for an endplay on West.

Bellis won the heart lead and cashed the king of clubs, West throwing a diamond. After a club to the ace he turned to the spade suit. Five rounds of spades brought him to this position:

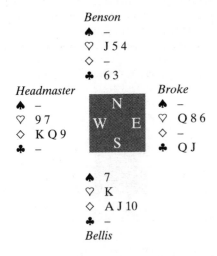

Benson
♠ —
♡ J 5 4
♢ —
♣ 6 3

Headmaster
♠ —
♡ 9 7
♢ K Q 9
♣ —

Broke
♠ —
♡ Q 8 6
♢ —
♣ Q J

Bellis
♠ 7
♡ K
♢ A J 10
♣ —

The Headmaster puffed thoughtfully on his pipe when declarer's last spade appeared. What now? If he threw a diamond, declarer would simply play ace and another diamond, setting up a twelfth trick in that suit. It seemed he would have to release a heart.

When ♡7 appeared on his left, Bertie Bellis proceeded to cash ♡K, reducing the Headmaster to three diamonds. He then exited with ♢J, forcing the Headmaster to win with one honour and lead away from the other. Twelve tricks had been made.

'At first I thought I should have left it in Six Spades,' Bellis observed. 'A diamond lead puts that three down on a crossruff, as it happens.'

The Headmaster glared across the table. 'That's another bottom for us!' he exclaimed.

Broke looked back nervously. 'Sorry, Sir,' he said.

'Had I not opened 4◊, he would have hoped to find one of the diamond honours onside and gone down,' continued the Headmaster. 'With a hopeless partner sitting opposite, the bid was forced upon me. I could hardly allow Bertie and Percy a free run.'

'No, Sir. Sorry, Sir.'

The Headmaster moved his pipe from one side of his mouth to the other. It was typical of his luck that Bertie should hold all the cards and have the chance of doing something clever. Was there any law against a few good cards coming his own way? It was obvious he would fare poorly in defence, with this useless boy opposite.

A few moments later, Bertie Bellis was in yet another slam.

```
Love All                     ♠ 2
Dealer South                 ♡ K Q J 8 5 3
                             ◊ A K 5
                             ♣ K 9 3

  ♠ A Q 10 8 6 5      N        ♠ J 7 3
  ♡ 10 9          W       E    ♡ 7 6
  ◊ 10 8 6            S        ◊ 9 4 3 2
  ♣ Q 6                        ♣ J 10 7 5

                             ♠ K 9 4
                             ♡ A 4 2
                             ◊ Q J 7
                             ♣ A 8 4 2
```

WEST	NORTH	EAST	SOUTH
Head-	Reverend	Rupert	Bertie
master	Benson	Broke	Bellis
–	–	–	1NT
2♠	4NT	Pass	5♡
Pass	6♡	End	

The Reverend Benson paid scant respect to the Headmaster's overcall, resorting immediately to Blackwood. Bertie Bellis was soon installed in Six Hearts and the Headmaster led ♡10.

'I wasn't going to let the Headmaster put me off,' Benson declared, smiling across the table as he laid out the dummy. 'It was obvious we could make a slam.'

'Ah yes, nice hand, Charles,' Bellis observed. Good grief, what overbidding! Even facing his maximum 14-count, it wasn't obvious where twelve tricks would come from.

Bellis won the trump lead with the king and led a careful ♡5 to the ace, pleased to see the suit break 2-2. An elimination ending might now be possible. Both defenders followed to three rounds of diamonds. The Headmaster would surely hold a six-card spade suit for his intervention on so few points. He could therefore hold at most a doubleton club. Bellis cashed the ace and king of clubs, leaving this position:

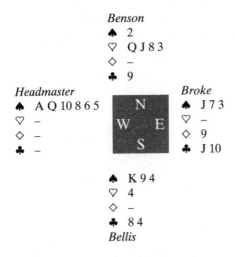

Benson
♠ 2
♡ Q J 8 3
♦ –
♣ 9

Headmaster
♠ A Q 10 8 6 5
♡ –
♦ –
♣ –

Broke
♠ J 7 3
♡ –
♦ 9
♣ J 10

♠ K 9 4
♡ 4
♦ –
♣ 8 4
Bellis

'Play the spade, please,' said Bertie Bellis.

Rupert Broke followed with the 3 and Bellis played a somewhat theatrical 4. The Headmaster, none too pleased at this development, had to win the trick. His only option then was to play the spade ace, hoping that declarer's king was bare. No such luck was forthcoming. Bellis ruffed with dummy's queen and reached his hand by overtaking ♡3 with the 4. 'They're all there now,' he said. 'Dummy's club loser goes on the king of spades.'

With a black expression the Headmaster seized Broke's curtain card. 'You had the jack of spades!' he thundered. 'Are you playing badly on purpose?'

'Of course not, Sir,' Broke replied. 'What should I have done?'

'Rise with the jack of spades, of course,' declared the Headmaster. 'That saves me from the endplay.'

'Move for the next round,' called a voice from across the room.

Broke could barely believe that they had played only one round out of eight. If the run of bad boards continued, a painful visit to the Headmaster's study would surely follow. What an ordeal! No wonder the experience had proved too much for Smithers minor.

5. The Matron's Successful Session

Madame Baguette drew deeply on her *Gitane*, then blew out a cloud of smoke. 'It's about the time we had a good result together, Matron,' she said.

Matron batted the smoke away. 'Yes, we've been below average five times running now,' she replied. 'That's unusually bad luck. It's like tossing a coin five times and finding every one comes down tails.'

Madame Baguette took a final drag on her cigarette, proceeding to stub it out in the staff-room ashtray. What did bad luck have to do with it? The Matron had little idea about bidding, even less on how to play the cards. Unfortunately, once you had formed a partnership it was difficult to escape from it. Perhaps she should abandon the game for a while and allow the Matron to find some other victim. Then she could make a surreptitious return. Phillip Glasson would probably have tired of the Goutier trollop by then. So tall he was and such an upper body! Just her type of man, in fact.

'Time to head for the game, I think,' said the Matron, rising to her feet.

The school duplicate was soon under way. Round 5 saw the arrival at the Matron's table of two tall sixth-formers. 'Hullo, Matron,' said the blond-haired Stephen Sutcliffe, pulling back the South chair. 'You and Madame Baguette having a good session?'

'I've no idea,' replied the Matron. 'I know you boys like to estimate your scores, but I don't see any point in it myself.'

The players drew their cards for this deal:

Game All
Dealer South

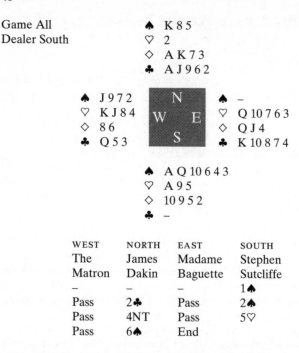

```
                    ♠  K 8 5
                    ♡  2
                    ♢  A K 7 3
                    ♣  A J 9 6 2

    ♠  J 9 7 2          N          ♠  –
    ♡  K J 8 4                     ♡  Q 10 7 6 3
    ♢  8 6          W       E      ♢  Q J 4
    ♣  Q 5 3                       ♣  K 10 8 7 4
                        S

                    ♠  A Q 10 6 4 3
                    ♡  A 9 5
                    ♢  10 9 5 2
                    ♣  –
```

WEST	NORTH	EAST	SOUTH
The	James	Madame	Stephen
Matron	Dakin	Baguette	Sutcliffe
–	–	–	1♠
Pass	2♣	Pass	2♠
Pass	4NT	Pass	5♡
Pass	6♠	End	

The Matron thumbed through her cards. What should she lead? The unbid suits were hearts and diamonds but no sensible player would lead away from a king. No, it would have to be a diamond.

Sutcliffe won the ◇8 lead with dummy's ace and called for the king of trumps. Prospects took a turn for the worse when East showed out. He had four side-suit winners, plus one trump trick already made. To bump the total to twelve, he would have to score his remaining seven trumps separately, on a crossruff.

Sutcliffe played a heart to the ace and ruffed a heart. When he called for a low club from dummy, the capacious Madame Baguette paused to consider her play. Could South hold the queen of clubs? Surely not, or he would have taken a finesse in the suit. Eventually she held off the king and Sutcliffe ruffed in the South hand. West followed suit when a diamond was played to the king and declarer now cashed the club ace, throwing a diamond. A second club ruff was followed by a ruff of declarer's last heart. The lead was in dummy in this end position:

Dakin
♠ –
♡ –
◇ 7 3
♣ J 9

Matron
♠ J 9 7
♡ K
◇ –
♣ –

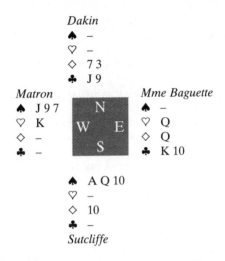

Mme Baguette
♠ –
♡ Q
◇ Q
♣ K 10

♠ A Q 10
♡ –
◇ 10
♣ –
Sutcliffe

When Sutcliffe called for ♣9, Madame Baguette followed with the 10. It was clear from her earlier hesitation that she also held the club king. Realising that if he attempted a ruff with the 10 he would be overruffed, Sutcliffe ruffed with the ace.

The Matron studied her remaining cards uncertainly. It seemed that she was caught in some sort of squeeze. She could hardly throw the king of hearts. No, the queen had not yet appeared and must be in declarer's hand to make up his twelve points for an opening bid. Perhaps she should throw a low trump? Yes, that must be it. Her jack of trumps would still be guarded, so she would have both suits under control.

Stephen Sutcliffe could not believe it when a trump appeared from the Matron's hand. Had she kept three trumps, she would have had to ruff his diamond exit and lead into the Q 10 of trumps! When declarer played ◇10 the Matron threw the heart king and Madame Baguette won with the queen. Matron's jack of trumps scored the setting trick and the slam was one down.

'How many points did you have, young man?' demanded the Matron. 'I could have thrown the king of hearts earlier, as it happens. I thought you must hold the queen.'

The young declarer reached for his curtain card and passed it for the Matron's inspection.

'That's a Weak Two opening, not a one-bid,' the Matron exclaimed. 'A one-bid on ten points, whatever next? No wonder you youngsters get too high all the time!'

A round or two later Matron and Madame Baguette took the
North–South seats at Table 8. 'Seems we have no-one to play against,'
observed the Matron. 'Ah, here comes the Headmaster. He and
Charles always take an age to move between rounds.'

'Welcome to our table, Headmaster!' declared Madame Baguette.
'For once in a while, the Matron and I are enjoying quite a good
session.'

'I'm pleased to hear it,' replied the Headmaster, taking his seat. 'A
happy staff makes for a happy school.'

Madame Baguette gave the Headmaster a conspiratorial smile. 'In
that case, perhaps you will give us two good boards more,' she
suggested.

The Headmaster shook his head. 'Too much happiness can lead to
complacency,' he replied. 'Now, who's to speak first on this one?'

East–West game
Dealer South

```
                 ♠  9 7 6 2
                 ♡  A 10 5
                 ◇  6 5 4 2
                 ♣  K 7

♠ K J 8 4              N              ♠ A Q 10 3
♡ Q J 9 8 3       W         E         ♡ 7 6 2
◇ A 7                                 ◇ –
♣ A 5                  S              ♣ Q J 10 8 4 2

                 ♠  5
                 ♡  K 4
                 ◇  K Q J 10 9 8 3
                 ♣  9 6 3
```

WEST	NORTH	EAST	SOUTH
Head-	The	Reverend	Madame
master	Matron	Benson	Baguette
–	–	–	3◇
Dble	Pass	4◇	Pass
4♡	5◇	Dble	End

The Matron passed on the first round, hoping that the near-senile
school chaplain might misunderstand the Headmaster's double. When
the opponents sailed into a heart game, she was in no doubt where her
duty lay. Four-card support for a weak pre-empt, and the opponents
vulnerable? It was obvious to sacrifice. She wouldn't be put off by
Charles's 4◇ bid. No, that was an obvious psyche.

The Headmaster led ♡Q against the doubled diamond game and down went the dummy. 'Thank you very much, partner!' exclaimed Madame Baguette. 'Small, please.'

She won the ♡Q lead with the king and took an immediate finesse of dummy's ♡10. When this succeeded, she discarded her spade loser on the heart ace. These preliminaries at an end, it was time to play on trumps. The Headmaster eventually scored his minor-suit aces, but that was all.

'You made eleven tricks?' queried the Matron. 'It's a *very* cheap sacrifice in that case!'

Madame Baguette nodded. 'We were lucky with the lead,' she observed. 'Any other lead and I don't think I can make it.'

The Headmaster glared across the table. 'How can I imagine you have no heart honour, Charles?' he exclaimed. 'Don't make a fatuous cue-bid next time. Bid the obvious Four Spades.'

The long-suffering Reverend Benson returned his cards to the wallet. Yet again, it had all been his fault. During thirty years at the table, the Headmaster had never once made a mistake himself.

'Bid Four Spades and I lead a spade,' persisted the Headmaster.

'One pair went down in Four Diamonds doubled,' observed the Matron, who was filling out the score-sheet.

'That's totally impossible,' declared the Headmaster. 'Some younger boy messing around, it must have been. Spoiling the game for everyone else.'

'I think ace and another club might hold them to nine tricks,' said Benson. 'When you win with the ace of trumps, you cross to my hand in spades and score a ruff with the seven of trumps.'

'The dummy's trumps were headed by the six, Headmaster,' said Madame Baguette. 'Do you see? Your seven would win the trick.'

'If Charles responds 4♣ to my double, I would lead a club,' declared the Headmaster. 'That's what must have happened at the other table. His cue-bid in diamonds didn't help me at all.'

Benson surveyed the four curtain cards learnedly. 'At double-dummy, declarer can prevent the club ruff,' he continued. 'He can play three rounds of hearts, throwing his spade away. You would have to win the third round, Headmaster.'

The Headmaster could not believe what he was hearing. How could Benson be such an expert in the *post mortem*, yet so totally useless during the actual play? It was a medical mystery that someone could suspend his senility just in one particular circumstance.

'I believe it's called a Scissors Coup,' said the Reverend Benson. 'Not that I've ever done one myself.'

The session was nearing its end when the Matron found herself facing two of the fourth-form's better players. She had noticed recently that some of the younger boys tended to snigger when they played against her. They took the game more seriously than she did, of course. Some of them could even remember a hand when it was over. In her opinion, though, playing too competitively spoilt the game. What did it matter who won? Bridge should be no more than a pleasant way of passing the time, similar to sitting in the garden on a sunny day.

The players drew their cards for this board:

East–West game   ♠ K 10
Dealer East   ♡ A 10 7 6 5 2
                     ◇ 5 3
                     ♣ K Q 5

	♠ 9 6 4		♠ 7
	♡ 9 3	N	♡ K Q J 8
W	◇ 10 8 6 4 2	E	◇ K Q J 7
	♣ 7 6 2	S	♣ A J 9 3

                  ♠ A Q J 8 5 3 2
                  ♡ 4
                  ◇ A 9
                  ♣ 10 8 4

WEST	NORTH	EAST	SOUTH
Madame	Neil	The	John
Baguette	Phillips	Matron	Hutson
–	–	1♣	4♠
Pass	4NT	Dble	5♣
Pass	6♠	Dble	End

The youngsters were soon in a slam and it was Madame Baguette to lead. 'Declarer has shown no aces?' she queried.

'No, we play ROPI when the Blackwood bid is doubled,' Neil Phillips replied. 'Redouble is 0 or 4 aces, Pass is 1. Partner's 5♣ showed two aces.'

'Why should we be interested in all that?' reprimanded the Matron. 'Do you think we're professionals?'

Madame Baguette led ♣7 against the spade slam and down went the dummy. 'King, please,' said John Hutson.

The Matron won with the ace and returned the king of diamonds, taken by South's ace. Declarer could count only ten top tricks and would therefore need to set up the heart suit. He crossed to the ace of hearts and ruffed a heart. A trump to the 10 was followed by a third round of hearts, ruffed high. West showed out but this caused no problem. Hutson returned to dummy with the king of trumps and ruffed another heart high. 'They're all there now,' he said. 'I can draw the last trump and cross to the queen of clubs to take two discards on the long hearts.'

The Matron blinked. The opponents had made a slam when she held 17 points? That was carrying bad luck to extremes. With 17 points she would have doubled them in game, let alone a slam.

Hutson turned towards the French mistress. 'Surprised you led a club,' he said. 'Matron's Lightner Double was a good effort. A diamond lead would have beaten it.'

The Matron looked uncertainly at the young declarer. What on earth was he talking about?

'Trump lead beats it too,' Neil Phillips observed. 'Takes an entry off the dummy.'

Madame Baguette waved these irrelevancies aside. 'Even on a club lead it should go down,' she declared. 'Hold up the club ace, Matron! How can he reach the hearts then?'

This was too much, even for the Matron. 'If you don't want me to play the ace of clubs, don't lead a club,' she retorted. 'This young man is quite right. After my er . . . Lightning Double, you should lead a diamond.'

The last round of the evening saw the Matron facing Bertie Bellis. She surveyed him with her usual vacant expression. Charming man, of course, but he had an annoying habit of playing well against her. 'I hope you won't get up to your usual tricks against us,' she said. 'You should take pity on two elderly ladies.'

Madame Baguette glared at the Matron. Elderly ladies? What a cheek! Why, the Matron was a good generation older than her. And Frenchwomen maintained their sexual attraction for a very long time – everyone knew that. In a suitable light, with make-up carefully applied, she could still pass for forty years old. Not much more than that, anyway.

Game All   ♠ A K 10
Dealer West   ♡ 8 6 5 4
                  ◇ A K Q
                  ♣ 10 5 4

♠ 7   ♠ Q 9 8 6 4 3
♡ A K Q 10 9 3 2   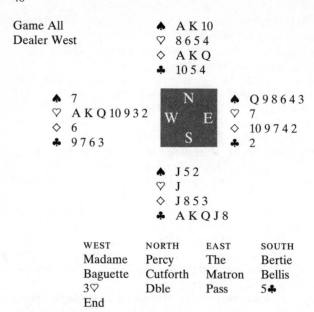   ♡ 7
◇ 6   ◇ 10 9 7 4 2
♣ 9 7 6 3   ♣ 2

                  ♠ J 5 2
                  ♡ J
                  ◇ J 8 5 3
                  ♣ A K Q J 8

WEST	NORTH	EAST	SOUTH
Madame	Percy	The	Bertie
Baguette	Cutforth	Matron	Bellis
3♡	Dble	Pass	5♣
End			

Percy Cutforth risked a take-out double of 3♡, despite holding no four-card suit outside hearts. The gamble seemed to have paid off when Bertie Bellis jumped to 5♣.

Madame Baguette led the ace of hearts, everyone following, and continued with the king. Bellis ruffed with the eight and cashed two rounds of trumps, East showing out on the second round. If declarer drew all of West's trumps he would have no entry to score ◇J. With the diamond suit blocked, and the spade finesse almost certain to be wrong, the contract was now in trouble. What could he do?

It took Bertie Bellis only a couple of seconds to spot the answer. He continued to draw trumps and, on the fourth round, discarded dummy's ace of spades!

The Matron looked suspiciously at the Maths master. He had thrown an ace away? That must cost a trick, surely, with her holding the queen. Was he trying to make fun of her?

Bertie Bellis crossed to dummy with ◇A and cashed the remaining top cards on view. This was the three-card ending:

Cutforth
♠ 10
♡ 8 6
◇ –
♣ –

Mme Baguette
♠ –
♡ K Q 10
◇ –
♣ –

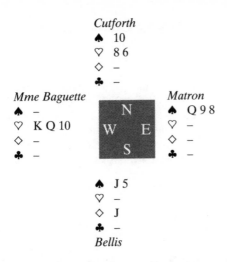

Matron
♠ Q 9 8
♡ –
◇ –
♣ –

♠ J 5
♡ –
◇ J
♣ –
Bellis

Bertie Bellis now demonstrated the worth of his spectacular discard in the spade suit. 'Play the spade ten,' he said.

The Matron had no answer to this. If she ducked, declarer would overtake with the jack and score a fourth diamond trick. Hoping that declarer held only one more spade, she chose instead to win the trick. Bertie Bellis faced his remaining two cards, claiming the contract.

The Matron was taken aback. How on earth did he know what cards she had left?

'A brilliant effort, Bertie,' exclaimed Percy Cutforth.

With a modest smile Bellis returned his cards to the wallet. 'That sort of entry-creating play is common enough in bridge books,' he replied. 'First time I've ever seen it at the table.'

6. The Spencer Grove Challenge

Cholmeley School stood at one end of Highgate Village. Near the other end was the Spencer Grove School for Girls. To prevent unseemly alliances, anywhere beyond the Highgate Post Office was out of bounds for Cholmeley boys. Similarly, the girls from Spencer Grove were not allowed to stray beyond the Post Office from their side. Many were the postage stamps bought during the course of a term.

'Would you credit it?' exclaimed the Headmaster. 'I've just had a phone call from Spencer Grove. Catherine Frowde has challenged us to a 24-board match.'

'How enjoyable!' exclaimed the Matron. 'I'd very much like to play in that.'

The Headmaster recoiled at the prospect. It would require a major epidemic before the Matron would enter into his team selection calculations.

The match was arranged for the following Thursday and the first set saw the Headmaster facing his opposite number from the girls' school, the well-endowed Miss Frowde. As was her custom, she was wearing a print dress that would have been the height of fashion some thirty years before.

'I see your A-level results were down this year, Headmaster,' said Miss Frowde, seeking to gain an early edge.

'Marginally,' the Headmaster replied. 'Yes, I was somewhat disappointed to see us only 8.4% ahead of Spencer Grove. It was the Classics department that let us down.'

The Reverend Benson, who taught sixth-form Latin, shifted uncomfortably in his seat.

This was the first board of the match:

Love All
Dealer South

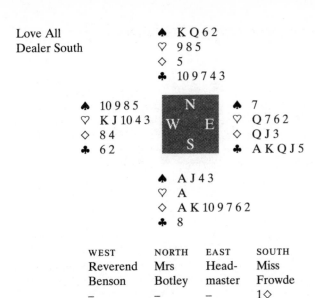

♠ K Q 6 2
♡ 9 8 5
♢ 5
♣ 10 9 7 4 3

♠ 10 9 8 5
♡ K J 10 4 3
♢ 8 4
♣ 6 2

♠ 7
♡ Q 7 6 2
♢ Q J 3
♣ A K Q J 5

♠ A J 4 3
♡ A
♢ A K 10 9 7 6 2
♣ 8

WEST	NORTH	EAST	SOUTH
Reverend	Mrs	Head-	Miss
Benson	Botley	master	Frowde
–	–	–	1♢
Pass	Pass	2♣	2♠
Pass	4♠	Pass	6♠
End			

The Headmaster bid 2♣ in the pass-out seat, thinking nothing of it. A few moments later, he was shocked to find himself defending a slam. He won the club lead and was quick to play a second high club, shortening the trumps in the South hand. Declarer would have to ruff the diamonds good, shortening the dummy's trumps too. If old Benson held four trumps, as seemed likely on the bidding, declarer might well lose trump control.

Miss Frowde cashed ♢A and ruffed a diamond. She then played two rounds of trumps, revealing the 4-1 break. At this stage West held two trumps, while she had one in each hand. These cards remained to be played:

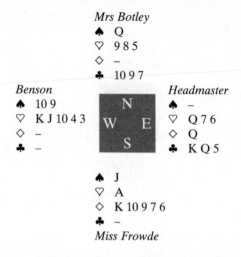

Mrs Botley
♠ Q
♡ 9 8 5
♢ –
♣ 10 9 7

Benson
♠ 10 9
♡ K J 10 4 3
♢ –
♣ –

Headmaster
♠ –
♡ Q 7 6
♢ Q
♣ K Q 5

♠ J
♡ A
♢ K 10 9 7 6
♣ –
Miss Frowde

When Miss Frowde ran her diamonds, there was nothing the Reverend Benson could do. If he allowed all five diamonds to pass, discarding hearts, declarer would throw hearts and clubs from dummy and crossruff the last two tricks. Benson chose, in fact, to ruff the diamond king. Miss Frowde overruffed with the dummy's queen, returned to her hand with ♡A, and drew the last trump. 'My hand is high,' she said, in a matter-of-fact tone.

The Reverend Benson gave an amused shake of the head. 'You should have let them play in One Diamond, Headmaster,' he said.

'Are you suggesting I should pass with fifteen points and a solid club suit?' demanded the Headmaster. 'Only a lunatic would pass on my hand.'

'As it happens, I don't think we can beat One Diamond,' continued the Reverend Benson. 'Still, it's a much lower-scoring contract.'

Meanwhile, at the other end of the staff common-room, Bertie Bellis had just arrived in a grand slam.

North–South game
Dealer North

♠ Q 7 3
♡ 8 3
♢ J 4
♣ A K Q 8 6 3

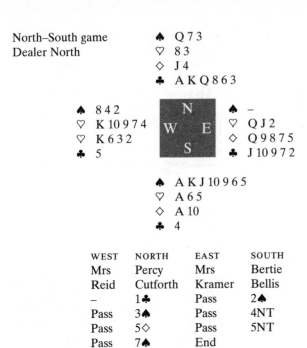

♠ 8 4 2
♡ K 10 9 7 4
♡ K 6 3 2
♣ 5

♠ –
♡ Q J 2
♢ Q 9 8 7 5
♣ J 10 9 7 2

♠ A K J 10 9 6 5
♡ A 6 5
♢ A 10
♣ 4

WEST	NORTH	EAST	SOUTH
Mrs	Percy	Mrs	Bertie
Reid	Cutforth	Kramer	Bellis
–	1♣	Pass	2♠
Pass	3♠	Pass	4NT
Pass	5♢	Pass	5NT
Pass	7♠	End	

The Blackwood 5NT king-enquiry confirmed that all four aces were
present. With a potential source of tricks in the club suit, Percy Cutforth
declined to show how many kings he held, preferring a direct leap to
7♠.

Hilda Reid, a Scotswoman who was head of the geography
department, did not like the sound of this. The Headmistress had not
bid a grand slam in living memory and would surely be in some lower
contract at the other table. Unless she and Betty could find a way to
beat the grand, it would be a big swing away.

Mrs Reid led a low trump, East showing out. Mindful of the need to
preserve entries to the dummy, Bertie Bellis won in hand with the nine.
The obvious route to thirteen tricks was to set up dummy's club suit. He
crossed to the ace of clubs and ruffed a club with the ace, West showing
out. Bellis smiled to himself. Thank goodness he had been careful at
Trick 1! He led the five of trumps and took the marked finesse of
dummy's seven. He then ruffed another low club with the king and
returned to dummy with the queen of trumps. 'They're all there now,'
he informed his opponents. 'I can throw these red-suit losers on the
good clubs.'

'Well played indeed, Bertie!' exclaimed Percy Cutforth. 'You go down if you win the first the trick with a lower card.'

Hilda Reid had been brought up in a Puritan household and could not stand opponents who congratulated themselves after every hand. 'That's not right,' she said. 'If you win the first trick with the five or the six, you can finesse dummy's seven on the second round.'

'Only if you play low,' Percy Cutforth replied. 'If you put in the eight, you would kill the second entry.'

Hilda Reid considered the matter. Good gracious, the man was right! The eight would force dummy's jack and the seven would no longer be an entry. Amazing.

Miss Frowde's notorious aversion to grand slams did not affect her appetite for the small slam bonus. Indeed, she had just bid her third small slam of the match. This was the deal:

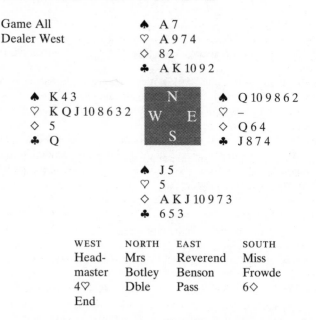

Game All
Dealer West

North
- ♠ A 7
- ♡ A 9 7 4
- ◇ 8 2
- ♣ A K 10 9 2

West
- ♠ K 4 3
- ♡ K Q J 10 8 6 3 2
- ◇ 5
- ♣ Q

East
- ♠ Q 10 9 8 6 2
- ♡ –
- ◇ Q 6 4
- ♣ J 8 7 4

South
- ♠ J 5
- ♡ 5
- ◇ A K J 10 9 7 3
- ♣ 6 5 3

WEST	NORTH	EAST	SOUTH
Head-	Mrs	Reverend	Miss
master	Botley	Benson	Frowde
4♡	Dble	Pass	6◇
End			

'Your partner's double?' queried the Headmaster, who was on lead.

Catherine Frowde seemed puzzled by the question. 'It's a penalty double, of course,' she replied. 'It could hardly be for take-out at the four level.'

The Headmaster led the king of hearts and down went the dummy. 'Not particularly good for diamonds, I'm afraid,' apologised Gertrude Botley. 'You may find these aces useful.'

'Thank you, Gertrude,' said Miss Frowde. Now, how should she play it? An old-fashioned player like the Headmaster would surely hold eight hearts for his opening bid. The first priority was to make sure that the ace of hearts wasn't ruffed. 'Small, please,' she said.

The Headmaster glanced respectfully to his right when the safety play became apparent. Still, he should expect no less. Anyone capable of rising to command in a large school was bound to be a player of near-international standard.

The Headmaster continued with the heart queen and Miss Frowde ruffed in the South hand. She drew one round of trumps with the ace, then crossed to dummy with a club, the queen showing from West. A trump to the jack won the next trick and she proceeded to draw East's last trump. West showed out when a second round of clubs was played. Miss Frowde won with dummy's king and cashed the ace of hearts, throwing a club. 'Ten of clubs, please,' she said.

The Reverend Benson's ♣J was caught in a ruffing finesse and the slam was now made. After ruffing East's jack of clubs, Miss Frowde crossed to the ace of spades and threw her spade loser on the established ♣9.

'Nicely played, Catherine,' Mrs Botley exclaimed. 'It was lucky for you that the defenders left that ace of spades intact.'

The Reverend Benson nodded his head emphatically. 'Yes,' he said. 'We needed a spade switch, Headmaster.'

The Headmaster glared across the table. 'If we needed a spade switch, you should ruff my heart lead and switch to a spade,' he said. 'I'm not going to switch from a king, obviously. You can see a spade is safe from your side of the table.'

Mrs Botley looked sympathetically at the elderly cleric. She knew what it was like, being blamed for every defence that went wrong. Headmasters and Headmistresses had one thing in common – they never made any mistakes at the bridge table.

After eight boards the Cholmeley staff led by 22 IMPs to 17. The second set had not been long under way when the Reverend Benson found himself in a difficult game.

Love All
Dealer West

```
                    ♠  10 5 3
                    ♡  Q 8 7
                    ◇  A K 9 2
                    ♣  8 4 2

   ♠  K Q J 9         N          ♠  8 7 6 2
   ♡  J 10 5 3                    ♡  –
   ◇  Q            W     E        ◇  J 10 8 7 4
   ♣  K J 9 3         S           ♣  10 7 6 5

                    ♠  A 4
                    ♡  A K 9 6 4 2
                    ◇  6 5 3
                    ♣  A Q
```

WEST	NORTH	EAST	SOUTH
Mrs	Head-	Mrs	Reverend
Reid	Master	Kramer	Benson
1♣	Pass	Pass	2♡
Pass	4♡	End	

Hilda Reid led ♠K and the Reverend Benson allowed this card to hold. He won the next round of spades and played a trump to the queen. 'That's unlucky,' he said, when East showed out, discarding a spade.

The Headmaster gritted his teeth. It was typical of old Benson to run into a bad trump break. The odds published in bridge books never seemed to apply when he was declarer.

Reverend Benson cashed the ace of diamonds, dropping the queen from West. Mindful that this might be a singleton, he crossed to the ace of trumps and led a second round of diamonds towards the king. There was no point in ruffing a loser with a winning trump, so Mrs Reid discarded a club. Taking advantage of his last entry to dummy, Benson ruffed dummy's remaining spade. He then exited with king and another trump, throwing West on lead. These cards were still to be played:

Headmaster
♠ –
♡ –
♢ 9 2
♣ 8 4

Mrs Reid
♠ J
♡ –
♢ –
♣ K J 9

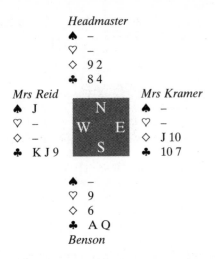

Mrs Kramer
♠ –
♡ –
♢ J 10
♣ 10 7

♠ –
♡ 9
♢ 6
♣ A Q

Benson

Not foreseeing any problem, Mrs Reid spun ♠J onto the table. Benson allowed this to hold, however, throwing a diamond loser from his hand. It was the end of the road for the defenders. West had to play a club into declarer's tenace and the game had been made.

Mrs Reid looked curiously at the cleric. 'That was cleverly played,' she said. 'I thought you were going down, there.'

'Yes, you played it very expertly,' said Mrs Kramer. 'We were told that the Maths master was your star player. If he's better than you, he must be some performer!'

The Headmaster could not believe what he was hearing. The first hand that Benson had played well in his entire life and these two women were hero-worshipping him? Had they not been impressed by the brilliance of his own performance? Few players would have escaped for one down in that diamond part-score a few moments ago.

'*Sapientia aetatecum crescet*,' observed Benson, basking in the attention he was receiving. 'I'm sure I don't need to translate for learned scholars such as yourselves.'

Mrs Reid and Mrs Kramer exchanged a brief glance. Latin, was it? What on earth was he talking about?

'It means: Wisdom increases with age, Headmaster,' continued Benson. 'The poet, Virgil, I believe.'

No doubt there was a similar ditty about the advance of senility, thought the Headmaster. In Benson's case, it seemed to have been gathering pace lately.

56

At the other table, with the first half drawing to a close, Miss Frowde found herself first to speak with this collection:

```
♠  7
♡  Q J 9 6 5 4 3
♢  10 9 8 4
♣  4
```

Normally she wouldn't dream of pre-empting on such a weak hand. The situation was quite different when her counterpart in the other room was an aggressive male. 'Three Hearts,' she said.

Bertie Bellis passed and Mrs Botley raised to Four Hearts, ending the bidding. Bellis, who was on lead, turned to his left. 'How do you play your pre-empts?' he enquired.

'Oh, very sound,' Mrs Botley replied. 'Particularly when we're vulnerable.'

Miss Frowde peered at the duplicate board. They were vulnerable, were they? She hadn't noticed.

This was the full deal:

```
North–South game        ♠  J 6 4 3
Dealer South            ♡  A
                        ♢  K Q 6 2
                        ♣  A 10 9 6

♠  K 9 8 5      N            ♠  A Q 10 2
♡  K 10 2    W     E         ♡  8 7
♢  J 3          S            ♢  A 7 5
♣  K J 5 2                   ♣  Q 8 7 3

                        ♠  7
                        ♡  Q J 9 6 5 4 3
                        ♢  10 9 8 4
                        ♣  4
```

WEST	NORTH	EAST	SOUTH
Bertie	Mrs	Percy	Miss
Bellis	Botley	Cutforth	Frowde
–	–	–	3♡
Pass	4♡	End	

Bertie Bellis led ♢J, covered by the king and ace. Miss Frowde won the diamond return and paused to consider her prospects. If she simply played the ace of trumps, returned to her hand with a club ruff and played the trump queen, the odds were high that the defenders would score a diamond ruff. Even if West held the trump king, he would be able to reach his partner's hand with a spade. What could be done?

Miss Frowde spotted a chance of countering the ruff. She crossed to the club ace and called for ♣10. When Percy Cutforth played low, she discarded her singleton spade. By swapping a spade loser for a club loser, she hoped to reduce the chance of suffering a diamond ruff.

Bellis won the club trick, and switched to a spade. Miss Frowde ruffed in the South hand, crossed to the ace of trumps, and returned to her hand with another spade ruff. The queen of trumps went to West's king and when declarer regained the lead she drew trumps and claimed the contract.

'Sorry, Bertie, I was asleep there,' Percy Cutforth declared. 'I should cover ♣10.'

'It doesn't help you unless you have two club honours,' said Miss Frowde. 'I can ruff, cross to the ace of trumps, and play ♣9.'

Bertie Bellis nodded. 'Yes, you played it well,' he said. 'I think you have to hold up the ace of diamonds at trick 1, Percy. Then I can use that as an entry for the ruff.'

Spencer Grove had moved into a 13-IMP lead as the teams broke for half-time refreshments. 'Time to assess the produce of the Upper Fifth's Domestic Science class,' declared Miss Frowde. 'This way, everyone!'

7. Bertie Bellis's Splendid Squeeze

The players from both teams were soon assembled in the Domestic Science Laboratory, where they would be served refreshments by girls from the Spencer Grove fifth form.

'You're not going to light that, are you?' said a horrified Miss Frowde.

The Headmaster, who had been filling his favourite pipe with Best Shag, looked up. 'Any reason why not?' he exclaimed.

'Smoking is out of the question in the presence of these young girls,' Miss Frowde replied. 'I only tolerate it in the staff room against my better judgement. Filthy habit!'

The Headmaster returned the pipe to his pocket. 'If some people had their way, all of life's pleasures would be banned,' he remarked.

'Girls!' cried Miss Frowde. 'You may bring in the food now.'

A line of neatly groomed fifth-formers appeared, each carrying a plate of delicacies.

'Buttered scone for you, Headmaster?' said Fiona Buckley, whose skirt was a good three inches shorter than the school regulations permitted.

'Very kind of you,' replied the Headmaster, selecting the largest scone with a practised eye. 'Do you play bridge yourself?'

The girl laughed. 'Not likely,' she replied. 'Boring game for oldies, isn't it?'

'Fiona!' cried Miss Frowde. 'How dare you be so rude to our guests. Go and er . . . get another pot of tea. I'm so sorry, Headmaster.'

The match restarted with a bang – Miss Frowde bidding her first grand slam for more than a decade.

Game All   ♠ A 3 2
Dealer West   ♡ J 2
                  ◇ A K 6 5 3
                  ♣ K J 5

West		East
♠ K Q J 10 9 8 6 5	N	♠ 7
♡ –	W E	♡ 8 7 4 3
◇ J 7	S	◇ Q 10 9 8 2
♣ 9 8 2		♣ Q 10 7

              ♠ 4
              ♡ A K Q 10 9 6 5
              ◇ 4
              ♣ A 6 4 3

WEST	NORTH	EAST	SOUTH
Head-	Mrs	Reverend	Miss
master	Botley	Benson	Frowde
3♠	3NT	Pass	4♣
Pass	4♠	Pass	7♡
End			

The Headmaster had been unable to follow the bidding. 'What did Four Clubs mean?' he enquired.

'Four Clubs is Gerber over no-trumps,' Mrs Botley replied. 'Everyone plays that, don't they?'

The Headmaster led ♠K and down went the dummy. 'Very nice, Gertrude,' Miss Frowde declared. 'Ace, please.'

At Trick 2 Miss Frowde called for a spade from dummy. The Reverend Benson looked at his two minor-suit holdings. If he threw a diamond, declarer might be able to set up dummy's diamond suit. Nor did it look a good idea to throw a club. Strange as it seemed, the best idea might be to play a trump. It was not as if his four small trumps could ever score a trick.

The Headmaster raised his eyes to the ceiling when a trump appeared from the Reverend Benson's hand. What was the old fool doing?

Miss Frowde overruffed and drew a round of trumps with the ace, West showing out. Dummy's two top diamonds, followed by a diamond ruff, revealed that the suit was 5-2 and could not be ruffed good. What now? Would she have to rely on the club finesse? A few moments' thought revealed a better idea. Miss Frowde ran her remaining trumps, arriving at this end position:

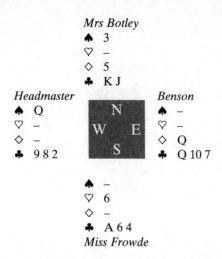

Mrs Botley
♠ 3
♡ –
♢ 5
♣ K J

Headmaster
♠ Q
♡ –
♢ –
♣ 9 8 2

Benson
♠ –
♡ –
♢ Q
♣ Q 10 7

♠ –
♡ 6
♢ –
♣ A 6 4
Miss Frowde

When the last trump was led, the Headmaster had to discard a club in order to retain his spade guard. 'I won't be needing that little spade any more,' declared Miss Frowde, waving a finger in the general direction of the dummy.

The Reverend Benson had to retain ◇Q to guard against dummy's ◇5. He, too, had to discard a club.

'I have them all now,' declared Miss Frowde, facing her cards. 'My last club is good.'

The Headmaster blinked in disbelief. What a freak of nature the woman was – she played bridge like a man! He peered across the Common Room, to the other table in play. Ah, good. With Bertie Bellis sitting South there was at least some chance of a flat board. Percy Cutforth never had a clue when it came to squeezes.

As it happens, Bertie Bellis was at that moment playing a quite different slam. This was the board:

```
North–South game          ♠  A J 7 3
Dealer South              ♡  A J 10 3
                          ◇  A 7
                          ♣  A 5 2

    ♠  K 9 5 2          N            ♠  Q 10 8 6
    ♡  8 7                           ♡  K Q 9 6
    ◇  6 4          W       E        ◇  5 2
    ♣  Q J 10 7 3       S            ♣  9 8 4

                          ♠  4
                          ♡  5 4 2
                          ◇  K Q J 10 9 8 3
                          ♣  K 6
```

WEST	NORTH	EAST	SOUTH
Mrs	Percy	Mrs	Bertie
Reid	Cutforth	Kramer	Bellis
–	–	–	3◇
Pass	6◇	End	

Bertie Bellis opened with a vulnerable pre-empt and Percy Cutforth decided to play for the jackpot, raising directly to Six Diamonds. Hilda Reid led ♣Q and Bellis won in hand with the king. Rather a wild fling by Percy, he thought, but the hands fitted excellently. If West had either or both of the heart honours, twelve tricks would be easy.

What could be done if East held both heart honours? Perhaps he could eliminate the other suits and endplay her. Yes, West's ♣Q lead suggested a sequence there, so it was quite possible she held five clubs, leaving East with only three.

Bertie Bellis crossed to the ace of spades and ruffed a spade with the 8. A trump to dummy's 7 permitted another spade ruff. Bellis then crossed to the ace of trumps and ruffed dummy's last spade, the suit breaking 4-4. The king and ace of clubs, followed by a club ruff, left this end position:

Cutforth
♠ –
♡ A J 10 3
◇ –
♣ –

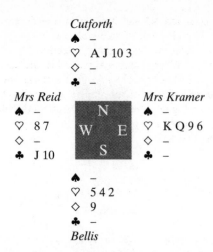

Mrs Reid
♠ –
♡ 8 7
◇ –
♣ J 10

Mrs Kramer
♠ –
♡ K Q 9 6
◇ –
♣ –

♠ –
♡ 5 4 2
◇ 9
♣ –

Bellis

Bertie Bellis now played a heart to the jack. The finesse lost but Mrs Kramer had to return a heart into the tenace. 'Annoying that you had that club sequence to lead, Hilda,' she said. 'Start with a heart and you kill the end-play.'

'Difficult lead to find,' her partner replied. 'If Catherine manages to reach the slam, I think she'll make it as well.'

Back at the other table Miss Frowde was about to play in 3NT.

Love All
Dealer West

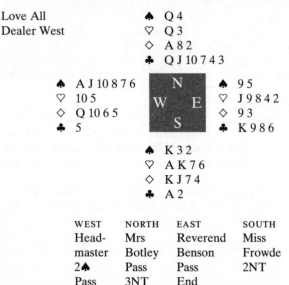

♠ Q 4
♡ Q 3
◇ A 8 2
♣ Q J 10 7 4 3

♠ A J 10 8 7 6
♡ 10 5
◇ Q 10 6 5
♣ 5

♠ 9 5
♡ J 9 8 4 2
◇ 9 3
♣ K 9 8 6

♠ K 3 2
♡ A K 7 6
◇ K J 7 4
♣ A 2

WEST	NORTH	EAST	SOUTH
Head-	Mrs	Reverend	Miss
master	Botley	Benson	Frowde
2♠	Pass	Pass	2NT
Pass	3NT	End	

The Headmaster led ♠J and down went the dummy. 'Thank you, Gertrude,' said Miss Frowde. 'Queen, please.'

Dummy's ♠Q won the first trick and declarer ran the other black queen successfully. When a club was played to the ace, West showed out, discarding ♡5. Miss Frowde had eight top tricks and was confident that she could land a ninth with an endplay. She cashed three rounds of hearts, West throwing two spades. She then crossed to dummy's ace of diamonds and surveyed this position:

Mrs Botley
♠ 4
♡ –
◇ 8 2
♣ J 10 7

Headmaster
♠ A 10 8
♡ –
◇ Q 10 6
♣ –

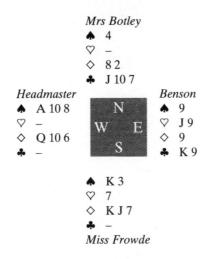

Benson
♠ 9
♡ J 9
◇ 9
♣ K 9

♠ K 3
♡ 7
◇ K J 7
♣ –
Miss Frowde

'Play the eight of diamonds, Gertrude,' said Miss Frowde.

West's hand could be counted as 6-2-4-1, so declarer knew she could guarantee the contract by covering East's card. When ◇9 appeared on her right, she played the jack. The Headmaster won with the queen and had to concede a trick with his return. He chose to return a diamond and Miss Frowde faced her K-7 tenace, claiming nine tricks.

The Headmaster had never seen a woman play the cards so efficiently. 'You did well to unblock dummy's ◇8,' he observed. 'If you lead the 2, to the 9, jack and queen, I can endplay dummy with the 8.'

'We have one or two third-formers who might make such an elementary mistake,' Miss Frowde replied. 'If any member of my staff were so careless, I'd want to know the reason why.'

With the boards beginning to run out, Bertie Bellis had been doing his best to conjure some IMPs in the plus column. He arrived in yet another slam on the penultimate board of the match.

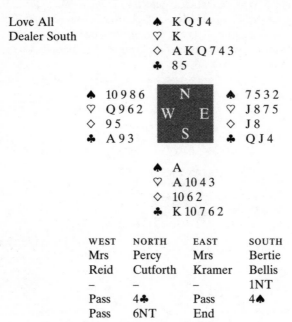

Love All
Dealer South

♠ K Q J 4
♡ K
◇ A K Q 7 4 3
♣ 8 5

♠ 10 9 8 6
♡ Q 9 6 2
◇ 9 5
♣ A 9 3

♠ 7 5 3 2
♡ J 8 7 5
◇ J 8
♣ Q J 4

♠ A
♡ A 10 4 3
◇ 10 6 2
♣ K 10 7 6 2

WEST	NORTH	EAST	SOUTH
Mrs	Percy	Mrs	Bertie
Reid	Cutforth	Kramer	Bellis
–	–	–	1NT
Pass	4♣	Pass	4♠
Pass	6NT	End	

Playing for a swing, Bertie Bellis ventured an off-beat weak no-trump. Percy Cutforth, feeling too exhausted for a scientific sequence, opted for a Gerber enquiry. When he heard of two aces opposite, he leapt to 6NT.

Hilda Reid led ♠10 and Bertie Bellis awaited the dummy with some anxiety. Now, how many tricks did he have? Six diamonds, four spades and two hearts. All was well!

Wait a minute, thought Bellis, this spade lead was awkward. Unless the jack of diamonds fell singleton, it seemed he would not be able to untangle his two heart winners. A 2-2 diamond break would not assist him, since if he used the third round of diamonds to reach the second heart winner, there would be no way back to the dummy.

Following the traditional remedy on such hands, Bellis decided to run some winners. Both defenders were under pressure when ♠J was led in this end position:

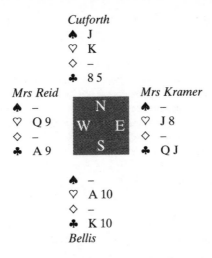

Cutforth
♠ J
♡ K
♢ –
♣ 8 5

Mrs Reid
♠ –
♡ Q 9
♢ –
♣ A 9

Mrs Kramer
♠ –
♡ J 8
♢ –
♣ Q J

♠ –
♡ A 10
♢ –
♣ K 10
Bellis

If East discarded a club honour, declarer would throw ♡10 and set up the slam-going trick in clubs. When Mrs Kramer threw ♡8, Bellis had some card-reading to do. If East held the club ace, he could simply discard a heart and lead towards the king of clubs. It was surely more likely that East had kept a guard on the club queen. Feeling he was on the right track, Bellis discarded ♣10.

Mrs Reid, who could tell she was the only defender with a heart guard, threw ♣9. Bellis now cashed dummy's ♡K and exited with a club. West had to win with the bare ace and concede the last trick to South's ace of hearts. The slam had been made.

'Masterful play, Bertie,' congratulated Cutforth. 'The communications might have been easier in Six Diamonds.'

'That's true,' Bellis replied. 'My ♣K had to be protected from the opening lead. That was the problem.'

The Cholmeley team had won the match by 7 IMPs and were soon returning home, through the lamp-lit Highgate Village.

'You were on brilliant form tonight, Bertie,' said Percy Cutforth. 'Your card-play alone must have been worth 40 IMPs.'

The Headmaster withdrew the pipe from his mouth. 'Are you forgetting the good boards at my table?' he said.

Percy Cutforth walked on in silence, trying to recall which boards the Headmaster was talking about.

'I don't think Miss Frowde will trouble us with another challenge,' the Headmaster continued, as the Cholmeley School chapel loomed out of the darkness. 'An intelligent woman like that must realise when she's outclassed.'

8. The Friendly Ladies Four

'Dolly Benson can't make it tonight,' said the Matron. 'She and Charles have tickets for *Il Trovatore* at Covent Garden.'

'She chooses a Wednesday, just to spoil our game?' exclaimed Madame Baguette. 'The opera is on every night, is it not?'

'We still have a four, don't worry,' replied the Matron. 'I have a pleasant surprise for you. Yvonne what's-her-name has agreed to play.'

Madame Baguette drew in air between her teeth. The Goutier girl hadn't the first idea about the game. What was worse, she had stolen the only good-looking man in the school. Phillip Glasson would surely have fallen for her own charms, had he not been bewitched by that young trollop and her short skirts. A disgrace to *la belle France*, that's what she was.

Later that evening, as soon as the boys were tucked up in bed, a rubber bridge session started in the Matron's room. The first cut placed the Matron in partnership with Yvonne Goutier. Madame Baguette would partner Molly Watts, school piano teacher and a lifelong spinster.

Love All
Dealer South

```
                    ♠ A 10 8 6
                    ♡ A Q 6
                    ◇ 10 7 3
                    ♣ K Q 9

  ♠ 4 3                        ♠ 5
  ♡ J 10 9 3 2      N          ♡ K 8 5
  ◇ 9 6          W     E       ◇ K Q J 4 2
  ♣ A 10 8 3        S          ♣ 7 6 5 2

                    ♠ K Q J 9 7 2
                    ♡ 7 4
                    ◇ A 8 5
                    ♣ J 4
```

WEST	NORTH	EAST	SOUTH
Madame	Yvonne	Molly	The
Baguette	Goutier	Watts	Matron
–	–	–	1♠
Pass	4♠	End	

The Matron rarely opened on fewer than 12 points but she had recently read that an exception could be made when you held a good 6-card suit. Throwing caution to one side, she hazarded a One Spade opening. Yvonne Goutier raised to game and ♡J was led.

'That's much too strong for a game raise,' observed Molly Watts, as the dummy went down. 'You should bid some other suit first, then bid 4♠ to invite a slam.'

'I 'ad no other suit to bid,' the French girl replied.

'That is a bit awkward, now you mention it,' said Molly Watts. 'I think I would have bid Blackwood on your hand.'

Matron played ♡Q from dummy, not thinking much of her luck when this lost to the king. Molly Watts switched to ◇K and the Matron could now have rescued herself by holding up the ace for one round. Such a play was not in her repertoire, however. She won immediately, drew trumps, and played a club to the jack and ace. Madame Baguette returned a diamond and two diamond tricks put the game one down.

The Matron sat back in her chair with a sigh. 'That's the last time I open on 11 points,' she exclaimed. 'One point extra in my hand and I'm sure I would have made it.'

Madame Baguette surveyed the Matron scornfully. 'You should have made it anyway,' she said. 'Win with the ace of hearts, draw trumps, and clear the club suit. That's the way to play it.'

The Matron could barely recall the hand. 'You may be right, as the cards lie,' she replied.

Molly Watts tapped the side of her long, thin nose. 'You have to know your opponents in this game,' she said. 'Madame Baguette never leads away from a king, so it was pointless to finesse ♡Q.'

Yvonne Goutier turned towards Molly Watts. 'Is it better if I 'ad bid the Blackwood, as you suggest?'

Molly Watts was taken aback. Such an innocent face the girl had. Surely she didn't mean to be rude. 'I don't think so, dear,' she replied.

The game proceeded, with the usual mixture of chatter and bridge, and barely an hour had passed when the score reached Game All.

Game All   ♠ A 8 2
Dealer South   ♡ 9 7
                 ♢ A J 8 7 2
                 ♣ A 7 2

```
      ♠ Q J              N          ♠ 9 5
      ♡ Q J 10 6 2   W       E      ♡ K 8 5 3
      ♢ 9 4                         ♢ K 6 5 3
      ♣ K 10 9 5         S          ♣ Q J 3
```

                 ♠ K 10 7 6 4 3
                 ♡ A 4
                 ♢ Q 10
                 ♣ 8 6 4

WEST	NORTH	EAST	SOUTH
Madame	Yvonne	Molly	The
Baguette	Goutier	Watts	Matron
–	–	–	2♠
Pass	4NT	Pass	5♢
Pass	5NT	Pass	6♢
Pass	6♠	End	

Madame Baguette led ♡Q and down went the dummy. 'Three aces facing a Strong Two-bid!' Yvonne Goutier announced proudly. 'If that is not enough for a slam, I do not know what is.'

Matron's mouth dropped. Strong Two-bid? Surely everyone played Weak Two-bids nowadays. Thank goodness they were only playing for penny-a-100 stakes.

She won the heart lead with the ace and led a trump to the queen and ace. She continued with another trump, pointedly playing the king from her hand. When the jack fell on her left, she turned towards Madame Baguette. 'Waste of time false-carding the queen against an old-timer like myself,' she informed her. 'I always play for the drop when the queen shows.'

Matron now led ♢Q. When West failed to 'cover an honour with an honour', it was clear that the king must be offside. She rose with dummy's ace and continued with ♢2. Molly Watts paused for a brief moment. Could Matron have another diamond? Surely not. She would have taken the diamond finesse in that case.

Molly Watts played low and shook her head in amazement when Matron's ♢10 won the trick. Noting the fall of ♢9, Matron returned to dummy with a trump and led ♢J. With a helpless shrug Molly Watts covered with the king.

'I have twelve tricks now,' said the Matron. 'I can cross to the ace of clubs and throw two of my losers on the good diamonds.'

'Win with the diamond king, partner, and you can cash a heart!' exclaimed Madame Baguette. 'How can you give them a slam when they don't even know what two-bids they are playing?'

'It was difficult for me,' Molly Watts replied. 'Matron played it very cleverly.'

A contradiction in terms if ever there was one, thought Madame Baguette. Why on earth had she agreed to play in a game of such an appalling standard? A few rubbers with three of the male teachers would have been more to her liking. Not that Englishmen were much use when it came to romance. Over two years she had been in this country and not once had she been propositioned. Could you believe it? Did Englishmen not recognise a beautiful woman when they saw one?

The next rubber placed the Matron and Madame Baguette together. This was the first deal:

Love All
Dealer South

```
                    ♠ Q 7 4
                    ♡ 6 4
                    ◇ A Q 7 3 2
                    ♣ K Q 7

     ♠ J 2              N           ♠ 10 9 8 6 3
     ♡ K Q J 10 8 7             W   ♡ 9
     ◇ K              W   E       E ◇ 9 8 6 4
     ♣ A 6 4 3            S          ♣ J 10 2

                    ♠ A K 5
                    ♡ A 5 3 2
                    ◇ J 10 5
                    ♣ 9 8 5
```

WEST	NORTH	EAST	SOUTH
Molly	The	Yvonne	Madame
Watts	Matron	Goutier	Baguette
–	–	–	1NT
2♡	3◇	Pass	3NT
End			

Molly Watts led ♡K against 3NT and continued the suit when the ace was held up. Madame Baguette won the second round of hearts, East throwing a spade, and led ◇J. Her eyes lit up when the king appeared on her left. She won with dummy's ace and played a diamond to the 10, preparing to claim the contract. This plan of action had to be abandoned when Molly Watts showed out, discarding ♣6.

There was no alternative to setting up the diamonds. When Madame Baguette ducked a diamond to East, Molly Watts completed her echo in clubs, playing the three. Yvonne Goutier won the third round of diamonds and, seemingly oblivious of her partner's signal in clubs, returned ♠10. 'I have the contract now, you foolish girl!' exclaimed Madame Baguette. 'You should have played a club to your partner's ace.'

Yvonne Goutier looked puzzled. 'You 'ad the club ace, partner?' she said. 'But you discouraged me in clubs. You played the six.'

Molly Watts did not like to be rude to a foreigner, but this really was too much. 'I played the six followed by the three,' she said. 'If that's not a come-on, even in your country, I don't know what is.'

'When Phillip is my partner, we play only the seven or 'igher is encouraging,' Yvonne Goutier declared.

'It was a comedy of errors all round,' declared the Matron, chuckling to herself. 'You shouldn't have led an honour on the first round of diamonds, partner. Make the safety play of leading the five and you bring in the whole diamond suit.'

Madame Baguette could not believe what she was hearing. 'What nonsense!' she exclaimed. 'When I lead the jack, I pick up single nine or eight with East. Leading the five picks up only one singleton, the king with West.'

'I dare say,' replied the Matron, 'but that's no excuse for missing the safety play.'

A hand or two later Madame Baguette had a chance to win a big rubber.

North–South game
Dealer East

```
                    ♠  A 6 2
                    ♡  9 8 5
                    ◇  A J 3
                    ♣  A Q 7 2

    ♠  9 8 4            N            ♠  7 5
    ♡  Q 7 4                         ♡  J 10 6 3
    ◇  6 5 2         W     E         ◇  Q 10 9 8 4
    ♣  J 10 6 4         S            ♣  9 8

                    ♠  K Q J 10 3
                    ♡  A K 2
                    ◇  K 7
                    ♣  K 5 3
```

WEST	NORTH	EAST	SOUTH
Molly	The	Yvonne	Madame
Watts	Matron	Goutier	Baguette
–	–	Pass	1♠
Pass	3♣	Pass	4NT
Pass	5♠	Pass	7NT
End			

'You bid 7NT, did you?' exclaimed Molly Watts.

Madame Baguette nodded impatiently. 'With my hand, it will be on top,' she said. 'It's your lead.'

Miss Watts led ♣4 and inspected the dummy disapprovingly. 'How can you jump-shift on that hand, Matron?' she exclaimed. 'You don't have 16 points.'

The Matron smiled benignly. 'Ah yes, but I have three aces,' she replied. 'I always add a point for that.'

Madame Baguette captured East's ♣8 with the king and proceeded to test the club suit. She shook her head in disbelief when it transpired that Molly Watts had led from J 10 6 4 in dummy's main suit. Had no-one ever taught her to look for a safe lead against no-trump slams?

When three rounds of spades were played, Molly Watts followed all the way and Yvonne Goutier discarded ◇10. Madame Baguette's spirits sank. Yvonne always gave true signals. It was obvious that ◇Q was offside and in that case it seemed that the grand slam could not be made.

On the fourth round of spades Molly Watts threw ◇2, confirming the lie of that suit. Delaying the fateful moment when she would have to take the failing diamond finesse, Madame Baguette played her last

72

spade. West threw another diamond, dummy a heart, and Yvonne Goutier had to release her heart guard in order to keep three diamonds. All followed to the king of diamonds, leaving these cards out:

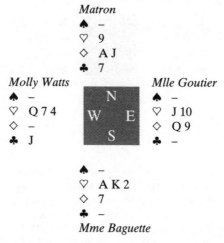

Matron
♠ –
♡ 9
◇ A J
♣ 7

Molly Watts
♠ –
♡ Q 7 4
◇ –
♣ J

Mlle Goutier
♠ –
♡ J 10
◇ Q 9
♣ –

♠ –
♡ A K 2
◇ 7
♣ –

Mme Baguette

'I can't believe this is going to work,' said Madame Baguette, steeling herself to take the diamond finesse.

Miss Watts confirmed this opinion by discarding a heart on the ◇7. Madame Baguette won with dummy's ◇A and scored two more tricks with the ace and king of hearts. Then, at Trick 13, a miracle occurred. She played ♡2 and neither of the defenders had a heart left! The grand slam had been made.

'You needed to hold on to the hearts,' Miss Watts informed her young partner. 'Still, never mind, it only cost one trick.'

'I could not,' Yvonne Goutier replied. 'You should 'old the 'earts yourself.'

Miss Watts struggled in vain to recall the hand. It was typical of today's youngsters to blame an older person for their own mistakes. 'I dare say you're right, dear,' she replied.

The third rubber, the last of the evening, placed the two French mistresses together. Madame Baguette turned a severe eye towards her young partner. How foolish she looked in that low-cut frock. It left nothing to the imagination at all. Had her mother never taught her how to dress sensibly?

The Matron reached game on the first deal of the rubber:

Love All ♠ 6
Dealer South ♡ 7 3
◇ A K 7 6 5 3
♣ J 10 5 4

♠ 9 8 5   N   ♠ K J 10 7 4 3
♡ Q 10 4   W   E   ♡ J 8 6
◇ Q J 9 4   S   ◇ –
♣ A 8 7   ♣ K Q 9 3

♠ A Q 2
♡ A K 9 5 2
◇ 10 8 2
♣ 6 2

WEST	NORTH	EAST	SOUTH
Yvonne	Molly	Madame	The
Goutier	Watts	Baguette	Matron
–	–	–	1♡
Pass	2◇	2♠	2NT
Pass	3◇	Pass	3NT
End			

Yvonne Goutier led ♠9 and Matron won the trick with the queen. Only eight points in the dummy? Surely Molly should have left 2NT with such a weak hand. For the contract to be made, the diamonds would have to break 2-2, obviously. Wait a moment, though. If she wasn't careful, her ◇10 would win the third round! Yes, even if the diamonds were 2-2, she would have to unblock the 10 and the eight on the first two rounds of the suit.

At Trick 2 the Matron led ◇10, covered by the queen and ace. She could not believe her bad luck when East showed out on this trick. Was a 2-2 break too much to ask for? The Matron continued with a low diamond to the eight. Yvonne Goutier was on the point of capturing with the nine when she realised that declarer would then be able to bring in the rest of the diamond suit. What if she allowed the eight to win? It was 'ard to calculate, but . . . yes, it did seem that the J-9 would stopper the suit.

Matron paused to take stock when her ◇8 was allowed to hold. She had two spade tricks and, now, three diamond tricks. If hearts broke 3-3 and she could score four more tricks from that quarter, she would actually make the contract!

The Matron played ace, king and another heart. The suit did break

3-3, she was pleased to see, and the third round was won by Yvonne Goutier's queen. Matron won the spade return with the ace and claimed the contract.

'Idiotic girl!' cried Madame Baguette. 'Why did you play a spade at the end? Once Matron has played ace, king and another heart, instead of ducking a heart, you can lock her in the dummy.'

'Did you not bid the spades?' Yvonne Goutier queried.

'Exit with a diamond or a club and we score at least four more tricks in the minors,' continued an aggravated Madame Baguette. 'Matron makes a silly mistake like that and you let her get away with it. This is meant to be bridge, we are playing?'

'I thought I played it rather well,' remarked the Matron. 'It wasn't an easy hand.'

The rubber had climbed to Game All when the Matron picked up this hand:

♠ K 7 3
♡ 4
♢ A Q 3
♣ Q J 10 9 6 4

It was very much a minimum, but nowadays people played a bold game. 'One Club,' said the Matron.

Molly Watts responded 1♢ and Madame Baguette entered with a take-out double. What now, thought the Matron. It was obvious that the opponents had a big heart fit. She would normally have rebid 2♣ but what had that column in *Children's Health Weekly* recommended? Over a take-out double you should bid one more than you would have done. Yes, that was it. 'Three Clubs,' said the Matron.

A few moments later, much to her surprise, the Matron was in a slam. This was the full deal:

Game All   ♠ A J 2
Dealer South   ♡ K 7
                 ◇ K 9 8 4
                 ♣ A 8 7 2

	♠ 985		♠ Q 10 6 4
	♡ 10 8 6 5 3 2		♡ A Q J 9
	◇ 6 5 2		◇ J 10 7
	♣ 5		♣ K 3

         ♠ K 7 3
         ♡ 4
         ◇ A Q 3
         ♣ Q J 10 9 6 4

WEST	NORTH	EAST	SOUTH
Yvonne	Molly	Madame	The
Goutier	Watts	Baguette	Matron
–	–	–	1♣
Pass	1◇	Dble	3♣
Pass	4NT	Pass	5◇
Pass	6♣	End	

Yvonne Goutier led ♠9 and down went the dummy. 'I was one point short of a 2◇ force,' Molly Watts explained. 'But I must be worth a slam try over your jump to 3♣.'

Matron studied the dummy disapprovingly. Molly Watts had never had much idea about bidding. Didn't she realise that 3♣ was pre-emptive?

After winning the first trick with the spade king, the Matron advanced the queen of trumps. She sighed heavily when the five appeared on her left. Yvonne would obviously have covered if she held the king. The only chance was to rise with the ace and hope that the king was singleton.

The Matron played dummy's ace but the king failed to drop. Prospects were dim indeed. Perhaps she could escape for one down if diamonds were 3-3 and she could discard her heart loser. When diamonds were played, both defenders followed to three rounds. The Matron triumphantly led the thirteenth diamond from the dummy. Everyone threw a heart and this position remained:

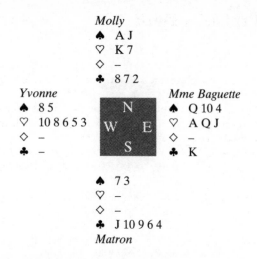

Molly
♠ A J
♡ K 7
♢ –
♣ 8 7 2

Yvonne
♠ 8 5
♡ 10 8 6 5 3
♢ –
♣ –

Mme Baguette
♠ Q 10 4
♡ A Q J
♢ –
♣ K

♠ 7 3
♡ –
♢ –
♣ J 10 9 6 4
Matron

Unwilling to lead from dummy's major-suit holdings, Matron called for a trump. Madame Baguette won with the king and was end-played. Since a spade would concede the slam even when declarer was now 1-1 in the majors, she attempted to cash ♡A. Matron ruffed and, after checking her calculations carefully, claimed the slam.

'Lead a heart, partner!' exclaimed Madame Baguette.

'But I 'ad six 'earts and only three spades,' Yvonne Goutier replied. 'I thought she would be short in the 'earts.'

'It was obvious to lead a heart,' Madame Baguette continued. 'You youngsters have such a lot to learn about the game.'

The Matron turned happily to her score-pad. 'The rubber comes to one shilling and sevenpence,' she announced.

'As much as that?' queried Madame Baguette. Thank goodness the hopeless Yvonne would not play again. A partner like that could bankrupt you in no time.

Molly Watts inspected her wrist-watch. 'Well, well, it's a quarter to eleven!' she said. 'Time for my beauty sleep.'

You've left it a bit late for that, thought Madame Baguette.

'I think we can all be very proud of how well we played,' said the Matron, rising to her feet. 'Not easy after a hard day's work, is it?'

9. The Cholmeley Flitch

'What is this er . . . Fleetch event?' asked Yvonne Goutier. 'You and I can be entering it?'

Phillip Glasson gave an amused chuckle. 'No, no, it's for married couples,' he replied. 'It's an English tradition, I don't think they play such events anywhere else in the world.'

'It does not surprise me,' the junior French mistress observed. 'The last person a woman would like to play bridge with is 'er 'usband, I would think.'

Glasson laughed. 'I quite agree,' he replied. 'Let's leave them at it and drive out to the Spaniards Pub for a few drinks.'

An hour or so later, the 1962 Cholmeley Flitch was under way. The first round saw Mr and Mrs Cummings facing the Headmaster and his wife.

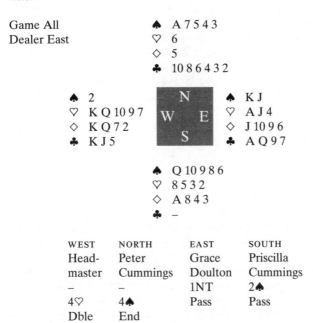

Game All
Dealer East

♠ A 7 5 4 3
♡ 6
♢ 5
♣ 10 8 6 4 3 2

♠ 2
♡ K Q 10 9 7
♢ K Q 7 2
♣ K J 5

♠ K J
♡ A J 4
♢ J 10 9 6
♣ A Q 9 7

♠ Q 10 9 8 6
♡ 8 5 3 2
♢ A 8 4 3
♣ –

WEST	NORTH	EAST	SOUTH
Head-	Peter	Grace	Priscilla
master	Cummings	Doulton	Cummings
–	–	1NT	2♠
4♡	4♠	Pass	Pass
Dble	End		

Priscilla Cummings was a large and vibrant woman, well known for her dashing tactics at the table. She overcalled 2♠, without even consulting the vulnerability, and was soon installed in 4♠ doubled.

Since his side had a considerable majority of the points, the Head-master made the best lead of a trump. 'Play the ace, Peter, darling,' said Mrs Cummings.

Peter Cummings, who was smaller than his wife in all respects, leaned forward to follow her beckoning. In an incident that had passed into school folklore, he had once been conducting the morning service in Big School. 'Let us pray for our shortcomings,' he had said. Schoolboys had long memories for such moments.

Mrs Cummings ruffed a club in her hand, cashed the ace of diamonds, and ruffed a diamond in dummy. Club ruff, diamond ruff, club ruff, left the lead in the South hand with these cards still to be played:

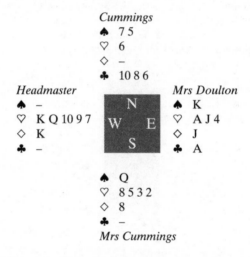

Cummings
♠ 7 5
♡ 6
♢ –
♣ 10 8 6

Headmaster
♠ –
♡ K Q 10 9 7
♢ K
♣ –

Mrs Doulton
♠ K
♡ A J 4
♢ J
♣ A

♠ Q
♡ 8 5 3 2
♢ 8
♣ –

Mrs Cummings

When Mrs Cummings led her last diamond, the king appeared from the Headmaster, sitting West. She was about to ruff the trick when a strange thought occurred to her. What if she discarded a heart instead! With no trump to play, the Headmaster would have to play a heart back.

Mrs Cummings followed this plan, discarding a heart from dummy on the fourth round of diamonds. The Headmaster's enforced heart return was ruffed in the dummy. Declarer could then crossruff twice more in clubs and hearts, making the contract.

'You made it?' exclaimed Peter Cummings. 'Well done, indeed. We only had 10 points between the hands, didn't we?'

'It was rather lucky,' his wife replied. 'If Grace had held the king of diamonds, I couldn't have ducked that diamond.'

Grace Doulton, whose enormous bun of hair would have been more appropriate in Victorian times, caught her husband's eye. 'I think you could have beaten it, Alfred,' she said. 'What if you unblock the king and queen of diamonds? I have the jack over here, so Priscilla wouldn't be able to duck into the safe hand.'

'What nonsense you talk,' the Headmaster replied. 'Unblock the king and queen? Priscilla might hold the jack.'

Round 4 saw the Doultons facing the favourites, the strong Bellis partnership. 'I hope you realise this is a social event, Bertie,' said Grace Doulton. 'Those clever plays you normally make would be quite out of place.'

Bellis smiled. 'I'll just play the card nearest my thumb, as usual,' he replied.

```
Game All              ♠  10
Dealer South          ♡  Q J 9 5 3
                      ◇  A 9 7 6
                      ♣  5 4 2

        ♠  9                        ♠  7 6 4 2
        ♡  8 7 6          N         ♡  A K 10 4 2
        ◇  K J 10 5 3   W   E       ◇  Q
        ♣  9 7 6 3         S        ♣  Q J 8

                      ♠  A K Q J 8 5 3
                      ♡  –
                      ◇  8 4 2
                      ♣  A K 10
```

WEST	NORTH	EAST	SOUTH
Grace	Bertie	Head-	Julie
Doulton	Bellis	master	Bellis
–	–	–	2♣
Pass	2♡	Pass	3♠
Pass	4◇	Pass	6♠
End			

Julie Bellis leapt to 3♠, to denote a solid suit. When her husband cue-bid in diamonds she cut short any further investigation and bid a small slam in spades.

Grace Doulton placed a top-of-nothing ♡8 on the table and down went the dummy. 'Nice hand, Bertie,' said Julie Bellis. 'Nine, please'

The Headmaster covered with the 10 and Mrs Bellis ruffed in the

South hand. A trump to the 10 was followed by the queen of hearts, covered and ruffed. Mrs Bellis drew trumps in three rounds and cashed her two top clubs. She then crossed to the ace of diamonds and led the jack of hearts. For the third time the Headmaster covered and Mrs Bellis ruffed in the South seat. It had been hard work, on declarer's part, but she had reached this end position:

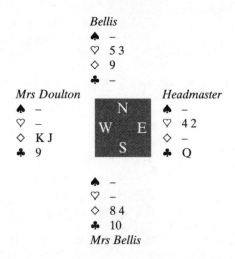

Julie Bellis exited with ♣10, throwing dummy's ◇9, and the Headmaster won with the queen. 'I can't believe the way this has turned out,' he exclaimed. 'I have to lead into dummy's heart tenace.'

Grace Doulton looked unsympathetically across the table. 'You might have tried unblocking the queen and jack of clubs,' she said. 'It wouldn't work, as it happens. Julie held the 10.'

The Headmaster did not take kindly to criticism of his play, particularly from his wife. 'It was obvious she had the 10,' he declared.

Bertie Bellis exchanged a brief glance with his wife. Had she spotted the brilliancy that the Headmaster had missed? Suppose, in the four-card ending, he had played ♡2 under dummy's jack! Declarer would then score one heart trick but not two.

'There was nothing we could do,' muttered the Headmaster.

The next round brought the Bensons to the Headmaster's table. Rumour had it that Dolly Benson played a better game than her husband, not that this was any great recommendation. Benson took hold of his wife's walking stick and helped her into the South chair. 'Sorry to delay you,' he said.

This was the first board of the round:

```
North–South game        ♠  A Q 7 4
Dealer East             ♡  9 3
                        ◇  K Q
                        ♣  Q 8 6 5 3

   ♠  J 10                        ♠  9 8 6 2
   ♡  A Q J 10 8 5     N          ♡  4
   ◇  9 7 5         W     E       ◇  J 10 6 4 2
   ♣  10 2             S          ♣  9 7 4

                        ♠  K 5 3
                        ♡  K 7 6 2
                        ◇  A 8 3
                        ♣  A K J
```

WEST	NORTH	EAST	SOUTH
Head-	Reverend	Grace	Dolly
master	Benson	Doulton	Benson
–	–	Pass	1♣
2♡	2♠	Pass	3NT
Pass	6♣	End	

'You alerted 1♣?' said the Headmaster, who was on lead.

'Yes, it's a Prepared Club,' Benson replied. 'Dolly doesn't like to open a weak major.'

The Headmaster thumbed through his cards. The king of hearts was obviously on his right, so a heart lead could be ruled out. As for the other three suits, there seemed to be little between them. Trump leads were for beginners and ditherers – he never led a trump if there was any reasonable alternative. Ah well, let's try a spade.

Dolly Benson wore exactly the same rimless glasses as her husband. Indeed, the two of them were so similar in appearance, they looked more like brother and sister than man and wife. She won the spade lead with dummy's ace and drew two rounds of trumps with the ace and king. After cashing dummy's two diamond winners, she returned to her hand with a third round of trumps and threw a heart on ◇A.

Dolly Benson paused to count the hand. The Headmaster had followed five times in the minors and surely had six hearts for his jump overcall. In that case he would have at most one spade remaining. A spade to the queen removed the Headmaster's last card outside the heart suit. This position had been reached:

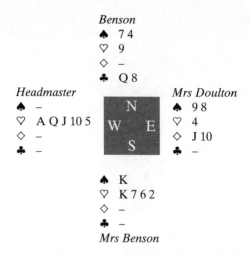

Benson
♠ 7 4
♡ 9
♢ –
♣ Q 8

Headmaster
♠ –
♡ A Q J 10 5
♢ –
♣ –

Mrs Doulton
♠ 9 8
♡ 4
♢ J 10
♣ –

♠ K
♡ K 7 6 2
♢ –
♣ –

Mrs Benson

'Play the heart, Charles,' said Mrs Benson. When the 4 appeared on her right, her eyes lit up. Just what the doctor ordered! She ran the nine and the Headmaster won with the 10. 'I think that's the end of the road, Alfred,' she said, facing her remaining cards. 'You have to play a heart from the ace, do you not?'

The Headmaster stared curiously at the elderly declarer. Where on earth had she learnt to play like that? Or was it some freak performance of a lifetime, held back for his benefit?

'You're playing *misère* tonight, Alfred!' exclaimed Grace Doulton. 'Lead the ace of hearts and you can give me a ruff.'

'The bidding marked the king of hearts with declarer,' the Headmaster replied. 'It was out of the question to lead the ace.'

The Reverend Benson nodded approvingly as he inspected the score-sheet. 'Everyone else in Six Clubs went down,' he reported.

'I'm not surprised,' remarked Grace Doulton. 'A heart lead stands out a mile.'

The Headmaster could feel his blood pressure rising. 'The other pairs all played it from the North hand,' he said, fighting hard to control himself. 'The defender with the singleton heart was on lead.'

Dolly Benson looked happily towards her husband. 'Serves them right for not playing a Prepared Club,' she said. 'It usually works to our advantage.'

A round or two later, Percy Cutforth and his wife, Jane, arrived at the Headmaster's table. A greater contrast between man and wife could not be imagined. Cutforth, with his thick lenses and enormous brow, was the epitome of studiousness. Jane, with her carefree manner and infectious laugh, never seemed to have a care in the world. The Headmaster looked across at the grim figure of Grace Doulton. If only he had been luckier in his own marriage.

'Is everyone ready?' asked Percy Cutforth.

Game All   ♠ A 10 5 2
Dealer North   ♡ J 9 6 3
                  ◇ 10 8 7 2
                  ♣ 9

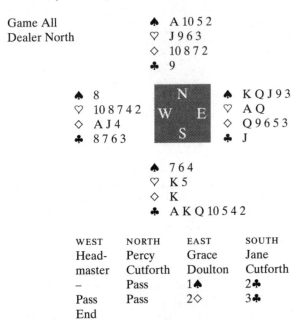

♠ 8   ♠ K Q J 9 3
♡ 10 8 7 4 2   ♡ A Q
◇ A J 4   ◇ Q 9 6 5 3
♣ 8 7 6 3   ♣ J

♠ 7 6 4
♡ K 5
◇ K
♣ A K Q 10 5 4 2

WEST	NORTH	EAST	SOUTH
Head-	Percy	Grace	Jane
master	Cutforth	Doulton	Cutforth
–	Pass	1♠	2♣
Pass	Pass	2◇	3♣
End			

The Headmaster led his singleton spade against a contract of 3♣. 'Ace, please,' said Jane Cutforth.

If declarer simply drew trumps now, she could not avoid the subsequent loss of five tricks in the side suits. Despite the risk of a trump promotion, she therefore had to risk the lead of a heart towards her king. Grace Doulton rose with the ace of hearts and cashed the king and queen of spades, the Headmaster pitching two hearts.

When Mrs Doulton persisted with ♠J, Jane Cutforth paused for thought. On the bidding, West surely held at least three trumps. If they were headed by the jack, a trump promotion could not be prevented. She therefore had to assume that East held ♣J. Ruffing the fourth round of spades with the 10 would lead to a promotion when West held four trumps to the eight. It must be at least as good to throw ◇K. Dummy's nine of trumps could then deal with a fifth round of spades.

Jane Cutforth discarded ◇K and the contract could no longer be beaten. Mrs Doulton did continue with yet another spade but this was

84

ruffed in the dummy, with the singleton 9. Declarer then reached her hand with a diamond ruff, drew trumps, and claimed the contract.

'Oh, very carefully played, Jane,' commended Percy Cutforth. 'I must show that one to Bertie.'

Once again, Grace Doulton looked aghast at her partner. 'We could have beaten it,' she said.

The Headmaster groaned inwardly. What was he meant to have done *this* time?

'Throw two diamonds on the king-queen of spades,' continued Grace Doulton. 'If Jane throws ◇K on the next spade, you throw ◇A! Then a diamond from me promotes a trump trick for you.'

'That's clever thinking, Grace,' said Jane Cutforth. 'I'm glad you weren't sitting West.'

'Had I been West, I would have raised to 3◇,' said Grace Doulton. 'Easy make, as the cards lie.'

The final round of the event brought Norris and Brenda Butcher to the Headmaster's table. A mundane part-score was followed by this slam deal:

```
North–South game        ♠ A K 5
Dealer South            ♡ A K J 8 6 4
                        ◇ 5
                        ♣ K 7 3

♠ 9 8 6            N            ♠ 10 4 3 2
♡ –           W        E        ♡ 10 9 3 2
◇ A Q J 10 6 4                  ◇ 9 8 2
♣ Q 10 9 2         S            ♣ J 4

                        ♠ Q J 7
                        ♡ Q 7 5
                        ◇ K 7 3
                        ♣ A 8 6 5
```

WEST	NORTH	EAST	SOUTH
Brenda	Grace	Norris	Head-
Butcher	Doulton	Butcher	master
–	–	–	1NT
Pass	2◇	Pass	2♡
Pass	4NT	Pass	5◇
Pass	6♡	End	

Brenda Butcher, who was smartly dressed in navy blue, led ♠9 against the Headmaster's slam.

'Alfred hasn't been in the best of form this afternoon,' said Grace Doulton, as she laid out the dummy. 'I was tempted to respond 6♡ immediately and play the hand myself!'

The Headmaster feigned amusement, hoping to dispel any thoughts that his wife had been serious. He won the spade lead in his hand and led a trump. On this trick Brenda Butcher looked meaningfully at her husband and threw ◇Q. The Headmaster had mixed thoughts when he saw this card. It was kind of Brenda to let him know that the top diamonds were sitting over his king. However, it wasn't at all obvious what he could do about it.

The Headmaster drew trumps in three more rounds, Brenda Butcher throwing two small diamonds and a spade. Two more rounds of spades revealed that West had started with 3-0 shape in the majors. From her signalling it seemed clear that she had started with at least A Q J 10 6 4 in the diamond suit. Prospects were poor if her shape was 3-0-7-3. If it was 3-0-6-4, a minor-suit squeeze might be possible. 'Play the rest of the trumps,' instructed the Headmaster.

This end position arose:

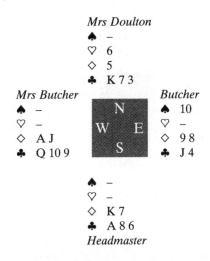

Mrs Doulton
♠ –
♡ 6
◇ 5
♣ K 7 3

Mrs Butcher
♠ –
♡ –
◇ A J
♣ Q 10 9

Butcher
♠ 10
♡ –
◇ 9 8
♣ J 4

Headmaster
♠ –
♡ –
◇ K 7
♣ A 8 6

Dummy's last trump drew ♠10 from East and ♣6 from South. The Headmaster turned to his left, awaiting West's card with interest.

'That's very awkward,' said Brenda Butcher. She detached ◇J from her hand, then pushed it back and reached for a club. No, that was no good, the Headmaster must have ace and another left in clubs. He would make three club tricks if she threw a club. Changing her mind yet again, she discarded ◇J.

His eyes bulging triumphantly, the Headmaster called for a diamond. The nine came from East and the Headmaster contributed the seven from his hand. With a helpless shake of the head, Brenda Butcher produced the ace of diamonds. Declarer's king was now good and the slam had been made.

'A squeeze without the count,' declared the Headmaster loudly. 'I don't expect anyone else will have found it.'

As was his intention, several players from adjoining tables overheard the remark and looked across.

'It required some delicate timing, Grace,' continued the Headmaster, in unabated tones. 'You were quite right to let me play it.'

Butcher turned towards the Headmaster. 'You seem to be in fine form tonight,' he said. 'Would it be presumptuous of me to assume that you were in the running to win the event?'

A loud snort came from Grace Doulton. 'If the winning score is less than 45% we may have a chance,' she retorted.

'I hear that the Bellis's haven't done very well, either,' Butcher continued. 'We played them on the last round and Bertie estimated his score at 53.27%. Rumour has it that Charlie Benson and Dollie are well over 60%. I don't think they've ever won it before.'

In need of consolation, the Headmaster reached for his tobacco pouch, proceeding to pack his pipe with Best Shag. Benson and his wife had not only finished ahead of him but were likely to win the event? If ever there was a final straw to make him give up the silly game, this was it.

He sucked his pipe into action and surveyed the throng of players through the gathering cloud of smoke. Well, perhaps he wouldn't give it up immediately. It would be nice to go out on a high note.

10. John Hutson's Memory Loss

The Headmaster looked across the table at the 82-year-old Reverend Benson. Doddering old fool, he thought. Just the sort of partner you didn't want in a Charity Pairs, with hundreds of master points at stake.

'Your bid, Charles,' said the Headmaster.

Reverend Benson, who had been on the point of dropping off, consulted his hand. 'One No-trump,' he said. This was the deal:

Love All
Dealer North

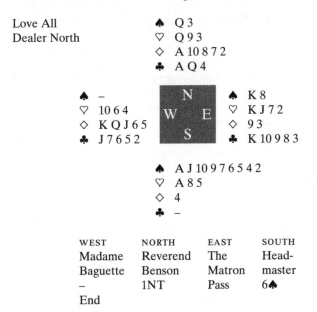

```
                    ♠  Q 3
                    ♡  Q 9 3
                    ◇  A 10 8 7 2
                    ♣  A Q 4

    ♠  –                        ♠  K 8
    ♡  10 6 4                   ♡  K J 7 2
    ◇  K Q J 6 5                ◇  9 3
    ♣  J 7 6 5 2                ♣  K 10 9 8 3

                    ♠  A J 10 9 7 6 5 4 2
                    ♡  A 8 5
                    ◇  4
                    ♣  –
```

WEST	NORTH	EAST	SOUTH
Madame	Reverend	The	Head-
Baguette	Benson	Matron	master
–	1NT	Pass	6♠
End			

It was the Headmaster's opinion that science rarely showed to advantage on freak hands. He leapt straight to 6♠ and Madame Baguette led ◇K. The Headmaster nodded contentedly as he inspected the dummy. 'Ace, please,' he said. 'And the ace of clubs.'

He discarded one heart loser on the club ace, then turned his attention to the trump suit. Everything would be easy if the suit divided 1-1, and if Matron held king doubleton in the suit she was a racing certainty to cover when the queen was led. Yes, against the present opponents the slam was an excellent one – a 75% proposition. 'Queen of trumps, please,' said the Headmaster.

Matron followed smoothly with ♠8 and the Headmaster confidently played the ace, preparing to face his remaining cards by way of claiming the contract. He could not believe it when West showed out and a few seconds later the slam was one down. 'You didn't cover with king doubleton, Matron?' he gasped.

'I always used to,' replied the Matron, looking pleased with herself. 'A recent bridge column in *Children's Health Weekly* advised to the contrary, however. I don't remember why, but it recommended not covering when a queen is led.'

'Perhaps it is for fooling the declarer,' Madame Baguette suggested. 'He will think the king is not with you.'

The Reverend Benson stirred in his seat. 'If you weren't intending to finesse in trumps, Headmaster,' he said, 'why not ruff a diamond at trick two?'

The Headmaster raised his eyes to the ceiling. Playing bridge with such poor players was more taxing than teaching Divinity to those renegades in Class 3C. 'Ruff a diamond?' he exclaimed. 'What possible use could that be?'

'Well, I may be wrong,' continued Reverend Benson, 'but when I saw Matron's ◇9 on the first trick it seemed that she might hold a doubleton in the suit. If you remove her second diamond, by ruffing one round, then perhaps when the king of trumps doesn't fall you can end-play her.'

'He's absolutely right, Headmaster,' declared Madame Baguette. 'Matron held the king of hearts, so a heart lead would run round to the queen.'

'Yes, round to dummy's queen,' said the Matron. 'Do you see, Headmaster? You wouldn't lose a heart trick at all.'

The Headmaster beckoned wearily for the next board to be brought into position. Being lectured on cardplay by the Matron was not exactly his idea of having a good time.

'And, of course, playing a club is no better,' continued the Matron. 'You see, Headmaster? It would run *into* the ace-queen and you'd be able to discard two hearts.'

The Reverend Benson suffered from arthritis and it was with some difficulty that he managed to unfold the travelling score-sheet. 'Hardly anyone bid the slam,' he reported. 'They all made twelve tricks, though.'

Matron smiled warmly at the French mistress. 'I'm so glad I didn't cover the queen,' she declared. 'It's a very sound publication, that *Children's Health Weekly*. You can always rely on what they tell you there.'

On the next round the Headmaster found himself facing Harry Walshe-Atkins, a distinctly lazy fifth-former who had failed to distinguish himself in any area of school activity. His father, an Old Cholmeleian, had made a fortune in the wine trade and was one of the school's most generous benefactors. The Headmaster had to bear this continually in mind when dealing with the young renegade.

The players drew their cards for this board:

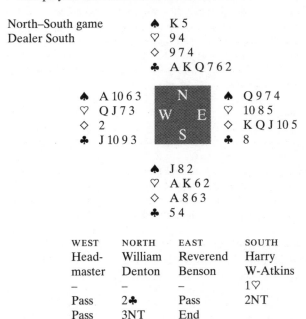

North–South game
Dealer South

```
                  ♠ K 5
                  ♡ 9 4
                  ◇ 9 7 4
                  ♣ A K Q 7 6 2

  ♠ A 10 6 3          N          ♠ Q 9 7 4
  ♡ Q J 7 3                      ♡ 10 8 5
  ◇ 2          W         E       ◇ K Q J 10 5
  ♣ J 10 9 3          S          ♣ 8

                  ♠ J 8 2
                  ♡ A K 6 2
                  ◇ A 8 6 3
                  ♣ 5 4
```

WEST	NORTH	EAST	SOUTH
Head-	William	Reverend	Harry
master	Denton	Benson	W-Atkins
–	–	–	1♡
Pass	2♣	Pass	2NT
Pass	3NT	End	

With two of his suits bid against him, the Headmaster decided to lead ♠3. Walshe-Atkins called for dummy's king, which won the trick. He then turned towards Reverend Benson. 'Fourth best?' he enquired.

Benson had no great liking for Walshe-Atkins. His lacklustre efforts in the 5D Latin class were bad enough, but there was no excuse at all for his present lack of civility. Had the word 'Sir' gone out of fashion? 'Two adjectives do not make a sentence, Walshe-Atkins,' the cleric reprimanded. 'A subject and a main verb are required, as in: Are you playing fourth-best leads, Sir?'

The Headmaster sent Benson a warning glance. Had he forgotten who had agreed to fund the re-panelling of the Dyne Library? 'I think we can save the grammatical instruction for another time, Charles,' he said, summoning a cheery smile. 'Yes, er . . . Harry, we are playing fourth-best leads.'

Concluding that the spades were probably 4-4, Walshe-Atkins decided to cater for a 4-1 break in the club suit.

'Small club,' he said.

Benson won with the singleton ♣8 and switched to ◇K. A few moments later, declarer had nine tricks before him: five clubs, the spade king, and three top cards in the red suits.

William Denton inspected the travelling score-sheet. 'Most pairs have gone down,' he reported. 'You played it well.'

The Reverend Benson leaned forward. 'It was very poorly played, in my opinion,' he said. '*Festina lente* at trick one, boy! Play low from dummy and you guarantee yourself a spade trick.'

'You might switch to diamonds, then,' said Walshe-Atkins. 'I wouldn't be able to duck a club.'

'You shouldn't duck a club anyway, not in a Pairs,' persisted Reverend Benson. 'The odds of a 3-2 break are – I forget the exact figure, you'll have to ask Mr Bellis – but it's something like 70%. You can't afford to throw away the overtrick 70% of the time.'

The Headmaster was sorely tempted to kick Benson under the table. Did he think that the Dyne Library would re-panel itself? 'Harry played it very astutely,' he observed. 'The hands selected for a Charity usually have a point of interest and, in the circumstances, a 4-1 club break was probably odds-on.'

The change of round was called and Walshe-Atkins rose to his feet. The Headmaster attempted another friendly smile. 'Give my regards to your father, next time you phone him.'

The next round saw the arrival of Bertie Bellis and Percy Cutforth. The Headmaster, who had been hoping to avoid this particular opposition, drew his cards for this board:

Love All
Dealer East

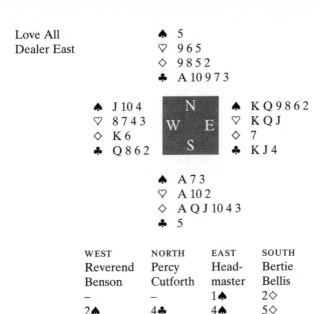

```
                    ♠  5
                    ♡  9 6 5
                    ◇  9 8 5 2
                    ♣  A 10 9 7 3

  ♠  J 10 4              N              ♠  K Q 9 8 6 2
  ♡  8 7 4 3        W         E         ♡  K Q J
  ◇  K 6                                ◇  7
  ♣  Q 8 6 2             S              ♣  K J 4

                    ♠  A 7 3
                    ♡  A 10 2
                    ◇  A Q J 10 4 3
                    ♣  5
```

WEST	NORTH	EAST	SOUTH
Reverend	Percy	Head-	Bertie
Benson	Cutforth	master	Bellis
–	–	1♠	2◇
2♠	4♣	4♠	5◇
End			

Benson led ♠J, his mouth falling open as he inspected the dummy. 'How can Gerber be right on a 4-count?' he exclaimed.

Percy Cutforth assumed a learned expression. 'My 4♣ bid is an invention of Bertie's, actually,' he replied. 'He calls it a fit-jump. It shows a diamond raise with a club side-suit.'

The Headmaster gave a disapproving shake of the head. What would the founding fathers of Acol think of these absurdly artificial methods?

Bertie Bellis won the spade lead with the ace and considered his prospects. Eleven tricks would be easy if the king of trumps was onside. If a trump trick had to be lost, he would need to set up dummy's club suit for a heart discard.

Bellis crossed to ♣A and ruffed a club with the 10. He then ruffed a spade and took a second club ruff with the jack. A further spade ruff allowed him to lead a fourth round of clubs. East discarded a spade and declarer ruffed high yet again, with the queen. These cards remained:

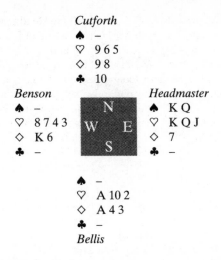

Cutforth
♠ —
♡ 9 6 5
♢ 9 8
♣ 10

Benson
♠ —
♡ 8 7 4 3
♢ K 6
♣ —

Headmaster
♠ K Q
♡ K Q J
♢ 7
♣ —

♠ —
♡ A 10 2
♢ A 4 3
♣ —

Bellis

Having ruffed with a trump honour three times, Bertie Bellis could now lead the 3 of trumps towards dummy's 9 8. Reverend Benson went in with the king of trumps and exited with a trump, won in the dummy. 'Just the eleven,' said Bellis, facing his remaining cards. 'One heart goes on the long club.'

'Lead a heart, partner!' exclaimed the Headmaster. 'He has no chance at all on a heart lead. I have the king-queen-jack over here.'

'You bid spades, didn't you?' queried Benson.

'Yes, yes, but we can score one spade trick at the most. It was obvious we'd need a trick or two from the heart suit.'

Percy Cutforth leaned forward helpfully. 'One of our special gadgets might have come to your rescue there, Headmaster.'

The Headmaster pretended not to hear, beckoning for the next board to be brought into position.

'Instead of bidding Four Spades, you could have bid Four Hearts,' persisted Cutforth.

'That's right,' agreed Bertie Bellis. 'To suggest a lead.'

The Headmaster flapped a dismissive hand at this suggestion. 'You can't expect Charles to play that sort of thing at his age,' he declared. 'Bid Four Hearts, indeed. He'd probably have left me there or bid a slam. Heaven knows what would have happened!'

Reverend Benson, who was hard of hearing, leaned forward. 'What did Percy say?' he enquired.

'Nothing, nothing,' replied the Headmaster. 'Bring up the next board, will you?'

Benson turned towards Percy Cutforth. 'If the Headmaster wanted a heart lead, he should have bid Four Hearts instead of Four Spades,' he said. 'Surprised you didn't point that out to him.'

The next round saw the Headmaster facing Butcher and Cummings, two members of the Modern Languages staff. Peter Cummings, who was shorter than most of the pupils he taught, was known for one rather eccentric habit. On games afternoons he would dress up in his old university sports gear. To the amusement of all onlookers he would then practise the high hurdles, running backwards and forwards across a sports field completely devoid of any hurdles. According to rumour, it was this impressive mating ritual that had first attracted the attention of his wife, Priscilla.

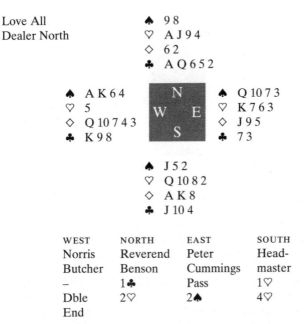

		♠	9 8
Love All		♡	A J 9 4
Dealer North		♦	6 2
		♣	A Q 6 5 2

```
        ♠  9 8
        ♡  A J 9 4
        ♦  6 2
        ♣  A Q 6 5 2

♠ A K 6 4          N          ♠ Q 10 7 3
♡ 5            W       E      ♡ K 7 6 3
♦ Q 10 7 4 3       S          ♦ J 9 5
♣ K 9 8                       ♣ 7 3

        ♠  J 5 2
        ♡  Q 10 8 2
        ♦  A K 8
        ♣  J 10 4
```

WEST	NORTH	EAST	SOUTH
Norris	Reverend	Peter	Head-
Butcher	Benson	Cummings	master
–	1♣	Pass	1♡
Dble	2♡	2♠	4♡
End			

The black-moustached Norris Butcher bore the air of a villain in a silent film. He led ♠A and down went the dummy. The Headmaster surveyed its contents disapprovingly. Since when did a barren 11-count constitute an opening bid? Still, if the club finesse was right ten tricks should be possible. The ill-considered opening bid might turn out luckily after all.

Receiving an encouraging signal from his partner, Norris Butcher continued to play spades. The Headmaster ruffed the third round in the dummy and crossed to ◇A. He then ran the queen of trumps, nodding approvingly when it won the trick. His expression changed somewhat when West discarded on the next round of trumps. What now?

If the Headmaster rose with dummy's ace of trumps and continued with the bare jack, East would win and play another spade, setting up a second trump trick for himself. 'Play the jack,' said the Headmaster.

Peter Cummings won with the king of trumps and paused to consider his continuation. This was the position:

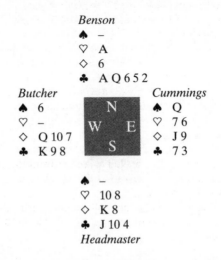

Benson
♠ —
♡ A
◇ 6
♣ A Q 6 5 2

Butcher
♠ 6
♡ —
◇ Q 10 7
♣ K 9 8

Cummings
♠ Q
♡ 7 6
◇ J 9
♣ 7 3

♠ —
♡ 10 8
◇ K 8
♣ J 10 4
Headmaster

A fourth round of spades would be unproductive. Declarer would ruff with dummy's ace, cross to ◇K, and draw trumps. He would then be able to pick up the club suit at leisure. Hoping to damage the Headmaster's entry situation, Cummings returned a diamond.

The Headmaster won with ◇K and played ♣J. All now depended on West's play to this trick. If he covered, declarer would win in the dummy, cash the ace of trumps, and return to his hand with ♣10 to draw the last trump.

Norris Butcher fingered his moustache thoughtfully. Cummings had signalled an odd number of diamonds. From the play of the trumps, that suit was obviously 1-4-4-4 around the table. Declarer had shown up with three spades, so his shape must be 3-4-3-3. With only J x x in clubs, he wouldn't have led the jack. He would have played low to queen, hoping for king doubleton in the West hand. Butcher nodded happily. Yes, declarer must have J 10 x in clubs. There was no point in covering.

When ♣J won the trick, the Headmaster took his last chance. He ruffed his diamond loser with the ace and called for the ace of clubs. If the king had fallen from West, he could have returned to his hand with ♣10 to draw East's trumps and claim the contract. When the king refused to drop, he was one down.

'I needed Norris to cover the club,' the Headmaster declared. 'Nothing I could do when he played low.'

Benson surveyed the travelling score-sheet. 'You must have misplayed it,' he said. 'Everyone else scored ten tricks.'

The Headmaster raised his eyes to the ceiling. Did Benson not realise how difficult the defenders had made it for him?

'Perhaps you should play the jack of trumps after ruffing the third spade,' Benson suggested. 'There's nothing they can do then, is there? If Peter ducks, you play the 9 of trumps. If he ducks that too, you cross to a diamond and play on clubs.'

The Headmaster could not be bothered to follow all this. Even if it made any sense, what was the point of being so expert in the *post mortem* when you were so completely useless at actually playing a hand?

'That's what I would have done,' said the Reverend Benson.

'Move for the last round,' called a Prefect from the far side of the room. Two fourth-formers arrived at the Headmaster's table. 'Is this table 12?' asked John Hutson.

The Headmaster picked up the table number card, affecting a close study. 'Let me see, there's a 1 followed by a 2,' he said. 'Yes, I believe this may be table 12.'

The two boys smiled politely, taking their seats.

The Reverend Benson emerged from a brief nap. 'Haven't they called the change of round yet?' he said.

The Headmaster sighed patiently. 'We played Norris and Peter on the last round, Charles,' he said. 'These boys are our next opponents.'

With the score at Game All, the Headmaster withdrew these cards from the wallet:

♠ K Q J 10 8
♡ K 10 4 3
♢ A 9 7
♣ 4

'One no-trump,' said Neil Phillips, on the Headmaster's left.
'No bid from me,' declared the Reverend Benson.
'Three no-trumps,' said John Hutson.

The Headmaster groaned inwardly. That was an unfortunate turn of events. Charles was bound to lead a club from some flimsy holding. Declarer would doubtless then knock out the ace of diamonds and run for home. Facing a strong partner, it would be obvious to double 3NT. This would ask him to lead his weakest suit, with the aim of hitting the strong suit held by the doubler. Perhaps he should risk a double anyway? A double could hardly be based just on high-card points, after such an auction.

'Double,' said the Headmaster.

Neil Phillips looked apprehensively to his right. 'Is that a lead-directing double, Headmaster?'

The Headmaster could not believe his good fortune. 'Technically you should ask my partner that question,' he replied, attempting a friendly smile. 'Still, I don't like to apply the rules too strictly against you boys. Yes, it's a lead-directing double, asking partner to try to find my strong suit. Usually this will mean that he leads his own weakest suit.'

'There's no need to shout,' said Reverend Benson. 'These boys aren't deaf.'

There was no further bidding and Benson led ♡9. This was the full deal:

Game All
Dealer South

```
              ♠ 5
              ♡ J 5 2
              ◇ K 10 8
              ♣ A Q J 8 7 3

♠ A 9 7 4 3         N          ♠ K Q J 10 8
♡ 9 7                          ♡ K 10 4 3
◇ 5 4 2        W       E       ◇ A 9 7
♣ 10 6 5            S          ♣ 4

              ♠ 6 2
              ♡ A Q 8 6
              ◇ Q J 6 3
              ♣ K 9 2
```

WEST	NORTH	EAST	SOUTH
Reverend	John	Head-	Neil
Benson	Hutson	master	Phillips
–	–	–	1NT
Pass	3NT	Dble	End

The young declarer called for dummy's ♡J, covered by the king and ace. Six clubs and two hearts would not be enough for the contract, Neil Phillips observed, so it seemed he would have to risk a finesse of ♡8. Still, Charlie B's top-of-nothing lead of ♡9 had denied the 10. The omens were good.

Phillips crossed to ♣J and led a heart. A finesse of the 8 succeeded and he noted with interest the fall of West's 7. When declarer ran the remainder of dummy's club suit, the Headmaster retained a guard on the king of hearts. It was to no avail. An eventual finesse of ♡6 gave declarer a doubled overtrick.

Hutson leaned forward excitedly. 'What did you have in spades, Neil?' he asked.

'I can't remember exactly,' Phillips replied. 'Two small, I think.'

Charles Benson looked helplessly across the table. 'Without your double I would lead a spade from ace to five,' he said. 'You were so insistent that I lead my shortest suit, I didn't see what else I could do.'

'Can you help me with the score, Headmaster?' said John Hutson. 'We've never made a doubled contract before.'

The Headmaster looked uncertainly at his young adversary. Was he being impertinent? 'It's 750,' he replied. 'You should be able to score at your age.'

'Does that include the overtrick, Headmaster?' asked Neil Phillips.

'You made an overtrick?' exclaimed the Headmaster. 'It's 950 in that case.'

The Headmaster gritted his teeth. The story would be all round the school before nightfall. Hopeless bidding by the boys, of course. Five Clubs was cold with the heart king onside. 'Don't go telling everyone about that last board,' he said. 'They'll just laugh at you for bidding so stupidly.'

John Hutson felt into the depths of his pocket, where he had already secreted the four precious curtain cards. 'Which board do you mean, Headmaster?' he asked innocently. 'I've forgotten about it already.'

11. After Lights-out

The summer term was due to end on the next day. Parents would arrive in their Rovers and BMWs, after long drives from various parts of the country. Tuck boxes and cricket bats would be carried out of School House and many fond farewells would be bid.

In the meantime a dormitory feast was about to start. For several days, bottles of beer and cider had been secreted under the floorboards of the fourth-form dormitory. Packets of crisps, nuts and pork scratchings had joined them.

'It's 11 o'clock,' Hutson whispered. 'Shall we make a start?'

A look-out was posted on the door and the first batch of bottles were opened. By the light of several well-positioned torches a night bridge game began on one of the beds. This was the first hand:

```
Love All                  ♠ 5 3
Dealer South              ♡ 8 6
                          ◇ Q 8 7 5 3 2
                          ♣ 8 7 3

        ♠ J 10 9 4 2        N          ♠ K Q 8 7
        ♡ 10 5 3       W         E      ♡ 9 4 2
        ◇ 9                 S          ◇ K 10 6
        ♣ J 9 6 5                      ♣ K 10 4

                          ♠ A 6
                          ♡ A K Q J 7
                          ◇ A J 4
                          ♣ A Q 2
```

WEST	NORTH	EAST	SOUTH
Neil	Julian	Rupert	Stuart
Phillips	Dyer	Broke	Melchett
–	–	–	2♣
Pass	2◇	Pass	2♡
Pass	2NT	Pass	3NT
Pass	4♡	End	

'Get a move on, Phillips!' said one of the onlookers. 'It's your lead.'

Phillips put down his bottle of Watney's Pale. 'I know!' he exclaimed. 'I was just thinking what to lead.'

The jack of spades was led and Julian Dyer put down the dummy. 'Could have left 3NT, I suppose,' he said.

'That's OK,' his partner replied. 'It's better in hearts.'

Melchett ducked the first round of spades and won the spade continuation. He drew trumps in three rounds, then led ◇J. East was not to be tempted and the jack won the trick. Melchett paused for thought. Had one of the defenders been clever enough to duck from king doubleton of diamonds? Surely not. If ◇K was still guarded, the only remaining chance was to play that defender for both minor-suit kings.

To tighten the end position, declarer's next move was to duck a club. East won and exited safely with a third round of spades, ruffed by declarer. This was the position:

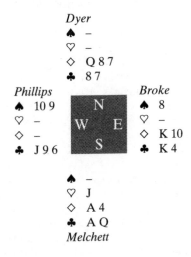

Dyer
♠ –
♡ –
◇ Q 8 7
♣ 8 7

Phillips
♠ 10 9
♡ –
◇ –
♣ J 9 6

Broke
♠ 8
♡ –
◇ K 10
♣ K 4

Melchett
♠ –
♡ J
◇ A 4
♣ A Q

Melchett led his last trump, throwing a diamond from dummy. Broke could see he was in trouble. He decided to keep his options open by releasing the last spade. When Melchett cashed the ace of clubs, Broke avoided the endplay by throwing the king under it. This would have saved the day, had West held the club queen. As it was, Melchett was able to face his hand, claiming the contract.

'Wow, that was a good one!' cried one of the onlookers.

'Shhh . . .' said seven other voices, as one.

The Headmaster rarely went to bed before midnight. If any noise was heard from one of the dormitories, retribution tended to be as swift as it was painful.

Soon afterwards, Melchett had a chance to win the first rubber.

North–South game
Dealer West

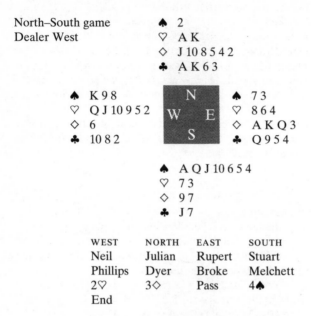

```
              ♠ 2
              ♡ A K
              ◇ J 10 8 5 4 2
              ♣ A K 6 3

   ♠ K 9 8                    ♠ 7 3
   ♡ Q J 10 9 5 2             ♡ 8 6 4
   ◇ 6                        ◇ A K Q 3
   ♣ 10 8 2                   ♣ Q 9 5 4

              ♠ A Q J 10 6 5 4
              ♡ 7 3
              ◇ 9 7
              ♣ J 7
```

WEST	NORTH	EAST	SOUTH
Neil	Julian	Rupert	Stuart
Phillips	Dyer	Broke	Melchett
2♡	3◇	Pass	4♠
End			

Phillips, who had opened with a Weak Two in hearts, led his singleton diamond against the spade game. Broke won with the diamond queen and cashed the ace of diamonds, West throwing a club. When East continued with ◇3, declarer ruffed with the queen and Phillips correctly declined to overruff, throwing a second club.

'Give me another beer,' said Melchett. 'I can't play properly with a dry throat.'

'You can't play properly anyway!' declared a voice from outside the ring of torchlight. An already-opened bottle of Murphy's Stout was passed to the declarer and play proceeded.

There was little point in a trump finesse, since West was marked with the king to make up the points for his Weak Two. When Melchett played the ace and jack of trumps instead, Neil Phillips won with the king and surveyed this position:

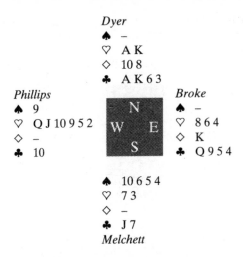

Dyer
- ♠ —
- ♡ A K
- ◇ 10 8
- ♣ A K 6 3

Phillips
- ♠ 9
- ♡ Q J 10 9 5 2
- ◇ —
- ♣ 10

Broke
- ♠ —
- ♡ 8 6 4
- ◇ K
- ♣ Q 9 5 4

Melchett
- ♠ 10 6 5 4
- ♡ 7 3
- ◇ —
- ♣ J 7

A heart was played to dummy's ace and Melchett now realised that he had no safe route to his hand. Resignedly, he played dummy's two top clubs. West ruffed the second of these and the game was one down.

'You twit!' exclaimed John Hutson, who was standing behind the declarer. 'You should cash two hearts and a club before playing another trump. He can't lock you in the dummy then.'

Melchett consoled himself with a deep draw on his bottle of Murphy's. 'I thought about it,' he replied.

'You liar,' said Hutson, laughing to himself.

'*Cave!*' came a harsh whisper from near the door. This traditional watchman's cry, the Latin for 'Beware!', signified the approach of a master. The cards were scooped up, half-empty beer bottles were grabbed, the torches were doused and empty crisp packets kicked under the beds. In under two seconds the silence of night reigned.

The door opened and the silhouette of the Headmaster could be made out against the corridor light. His eyes moved suspiciously from bed to bed, with none of the boys daring to breathe. Surely he had heard some noise. There seemed to be an unusual smell in the air, too. Ah well, perhaps he had imagined it.

The Headmaster departed and, after a wait of a couple of minutes, the game resumed.

East–West game
Dealer East

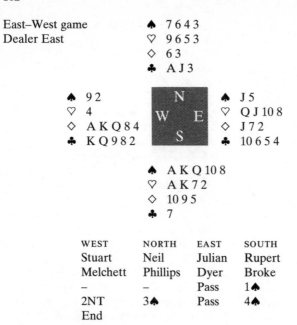

<pre>
                    ♠ 7 6 4 3
                    ♡ 9 6 5 3
                    ◇ 6 3
                    ♣ A J 3

  ♠ 9 2   N   ♠ J 5
  ♡ 4   ♡ Q J 10 8
  ◇ A K Q 8 4   W   E   ◇ J 7 2
  ♣ K Q 9 8 2   S   ♣ 10 6 5 4

                    ♠ A K Q 10 8
                    ♡ A K 7 2
                    ◇ 10 9 5
                    ♣ 7
</pre>

WEST	NORTH	EAST	SOUTH
Stuart	Neil	Julian	Rupert
Melchett	Phillips	Dyer	Broke
–	–	Pass	1♠
2NT	3♠	Pass	4♠
End			

Stuart Melchett, who had entered the auction with an Unusual 2NT, led ◇A against Four Spades.

'You didn't have much for that 3♠ bid,' said an onlooker, as the dummy went down.

'Couldn't pass with four spades, could I?' Phillips retorted.

Melchett cashed a second round of diamonds, then switched to ♣K. Broke won with dummy's ace and ruffed a club. He then drew trumps in two rounds and cashed the ace-king of hearts. The suit broke 4-1 but he was not discomfited in the least. He crossed to dummy with a diamond ruff and led dummy's ♣J, throwing a heart loser. West had to win and the enforced ruff-and-discard return allowed declarer to dispose of his remaining heart loser.

'Rubbish defence, Stuart,' said John Hutson. 'Play a third round of diamonds at trick 3! That takes away the entry he needed to exit with ♣J.'

Melchett reached for his beer bottle, tossing it to one side when he found it was empty. Play a third round of diamonds? It had never occurred to him.

'Doesn't make any difference,' said Broke. 'I draw trumps, test the hearts, then lead a club towards the jack. Stuart has to split his honours and I duck, leaving him on play.'

'Exactly!' declared Melchett. 'Surprised you didn't see that, Johnny.'

Hutson retaliated with a playful punch on the arm. 'Didn't notice you pointing it out either,' he said.

This was the next deal:

Game All
Dealer South

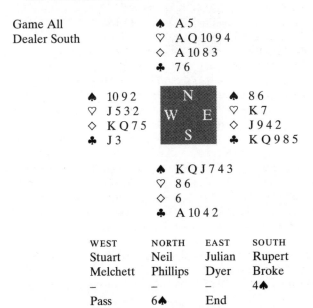

```
                  ♠ A 5
                  ♡ A Q 10 9 4
                  ◇ A 10 8 3
                  ♣ 7 6

      ♠ 10 9 2                      ♠ 8 6
      ♡ J 5 3 2         N           ♡ K 7
      ◇ K Q 7 5     W       E       ◇ J 9 4 2
      ♣ J 3             S           ♣ K Q 9 8 5

                  ♠ K Q J 7 4 3
                  ♡ 8 6
                  ◇ 6
                  ♣ A 10 4 2
```

WEST	NORTH	EAST	SOUTH
Stuart	Neil	Julian	Rupert
Melchett	Phillips	Dyer	Broke
–	–	–	4♠
Pass	6♠	End	

A beer-induced auction carried Broke to a small slam in spades. West led ◇K and declarer won in the dummy. A trump to the king was followed by a heart to the 9 and king. Julian Dyer peered at the dimly-lit dummy. What now? Did declarer have another diamond left? If not, there was a good chance that partner would hold ♣A. Which was it to be, a diamond or a club?

'Come on,' said a voice. 'We've been waiting ages to cut in.'

When Dyer eventually returned ♣K, Broke pounced with the ace. He crossed to the ace of trumps, returned to hand with a diamond ruff, and drew the outstanding trump. A heart to the 10 then set up dummy's heart suit. Away went three losing clubs and the slam was made.

Dyer shrugged his shoulders. 'Diamond back was no good either,' he said. 'I knew you held a singleton diamond when you blocked the trump suit like that.'

Broke laughed. 'You should play a heart back,' he said. 'It's two down, then. You kill the heart suit.'

'Heart back was obvious,' declared Hutson.

'Or you can hold up the king of hearts,' added Broke.

'That was obvious too,' said Hutson.

'Right!' cried Dyer, grabbing a pillow and landing some well-directed blows in Hutson's direction.

Suddenly the room was bathed in light. In the doorway stood the fearsome figure of the Headmaster, his eyes ablaze. 'What is the meaning of this, Dyer?' he demanded.

'Er . . . just an end of term bridge game, Sir,' Dyer replied.

'And these bottles?' persisted the Headmaster. 'These bottles, all over the place? You are aware of the rules concerning alcohol?'

'It's the last night of term, Sir,' Dyer pleaded.

The Headmaster flexed his right arm, preparing for action. 'You will report immediately to my study,' he declared. 'All eight of you.'

The Headmaster strode out of the dormitory and the boys looked apprehensively at each other.

'It's not fair,' said Keith Winterton. 'I was only drinking lemonade. I don't like beer.'

'And I didn't play a single hand,' complained John Hutson.

'Stop moaning,' declared Dyer. 'If you've got any sense, you'll put on an extra layer or two under your pyjamas.'

'I bags last place in the queue,' said Stuart Melchett. 'You never know your luck. His arm may be getting tired by then.'

12. Madame Baguette's Special Treat

The Headmaster regarded it as his duty to have the occasional bridge session with each member of staff. A duty for him it might be, he reflected, but of course it was a considerable pleasure for them. Not everyone had the opportunity of partnering a top-class player.

On the present occasion it was the senior French mistress, Madame Baguette, who had drawn the short straw. She eased her ample frame into the North seat. 'Strong no-trump, 3NT for take-out over the pre-empts, and ace from ace-king?' she enquired.

'Yes, yes, whatever you wish,' the Headmaster replied, nodding amiably. 'Mind you, I prefer the weak no-trump really. Let's play that.'

Madame Baguette gave a small sigh. What manners these English had! And how could they be so arrogant as to think the weak no-trump was a good idea. Did they not realise the rest of the world played a strong no-trump? Had not the French become world champions, playing such methods?

'And take-out doubles of pre-empts, if you don't mind,' continued the Headmaster. '3NT takes up so much space.'

'Perhaps you would like also to play king from ace-king?' said Madame Baguette huffily.

'No, no, whatever you prefer,' replied the Headmaster.

Bertie Bellis arrived at the table for the first round. His normal partner, Percy Cutforth, had a backlog of homework to mark, and on this occasion Bellis was partnered by the school Chaplain, the Reverend Benson.

The players drew their cards for this board:

Game All   ♠ A Q 9 7 2
Dealer South   ♡ 9 7
                ♢ 9 5 4
                ♣ 10 8 4

♠ 10 8 6 5		♠ K J 3
♡ Q 10 6 5 2	N	♡ A K 8 4
♢ J	W E	♢ 8 7 3 2
♣ J 7 5	S	♣ 6 2

                ♠ 4
                ♡ J 3
                ♢ A K Q 10 6
                ♣ A K Q 9 3

WEST	NORTH	EAST	SOUTH
Reverend	Madame	Bertie	Head-
Benson	Baguette	Bellis	master
–	–	–	1♢
Pass	1♠	Pass	3♣
Pass	3♠	Pass	4♣
Pass	4♢	Pass	5♢
End			

Reverend Benson led a fourth-best heart and down went the dummy. 'I think I would have bid 3♢ instead of 3♠ on that hand,' he observed.

Madame Baguette surveyed the white-haired cleric disdainfully. 'Five cards to ace-queen is not rebiddable?' she demanded.

'Yes, but 3♢ might allow you to stop at a safe level,' Benson replied. 'The 3♣ rebid is forcing to game, I realise, but if the Headmaster didn't quite have his bid he might welcome the chance to stop in a part-score.'

Madame Baguette gave an angry puff of the cheeks. It was ridiculous that someone so senile was still teaching. Back in her beloved France a *vide-tête* like him would have been put out to grass years ago.

Bertie Bellis won the first trick with ♡K and continued with the heart ace, his partner playing the 2 to indicate an original 5-card holding. What next? Perhaps declarer held A K J 10 x in the trump suit, leaving Benson with a singleton queen. On a passive club return declarer would make the safety play of cashing the ace of trumps, before crossing to the dummy to finesse against the trump queen. If

Benson did hold a singleton queen, the safety play would reap dividends.

A spade switch was beginning to look attractive. It would remove the only entry to dummy, forcing declarer to take any trump finesse on the first round. It could hardly cost, even if South was void in spades. A couple of club discards wouldn't help him very much.

The Headmaster was surprised to see ♠3 appear on the table. What on earth was Bertie up to, leading a spade into the tenace? Unless . . . Yes, there was only one explanation. He must hold four trumps to the jack! What a cunning devil Bertie was. Had he returned a club, there would have been time to cash two top trumps, exposing the 4-1 break; he could then have crossed to the spade ace to pick up Bertie's jack of trumps.

The Headmaster won the spade switch with dummy's queen and led the 10 of trumps, looking triumphantly at Bertie Bellis as he ran the card. He returned his eyes to the baize to find that the 10 had lost to West's jack. The diamond game was one down.

Madame Baguette glared across the table. 'You pulled the wrong card?' she exclaimed. 'Five cards missing to the jack and you finesse?'

'I certainly didn't expect to make my singleton jack,' chuckled Reverend Benson. 'I thought you'd blown the defence, Bertie, when you played that spade into strength.'

Madame Baguette filled out the score-sheet with exaggerated strokes of her pen. One down in such a contract! Even her regular partner, the Matron, would probably have made it.

The Reverend Benson leaned forward triumphantly. 'Remember what I said about the bidding?' he asked. 'A 3◇ rebid would have kept the bidding much lower.'

The next round saw the arrival of the Matron at the Headmaster's table. Deprived of her usual partner, she had persuaded Molly Watts to give duplicate a try.

North–South game
Dealer North

```
                    ♠ J 10 6 4
                    ♡ 4
                    ◇ A K Q J 4
                    ♣ A 8 2
```

```
♠ K 5 3 2           N           ♠ 7
♡ K 10 8 5      W       E       ♡ J 9 7 3 2
◇ 10 5              S           ◇ 8 6 3
♣ J 10 3                        ♣ Q 9 6 4
```

```
                    ♠ A Q 9 8
                    ♡ A Q 6
                    ◇ 9 7 2
                    ♣ K 7 5
```

WEST	NORTH	EAST	SOUTH
Head-	Molly	Madame	The
master	Watts	Baguette	Matron
–	1◇	Pass	1♠
Pass	3♠	Pass	4NT
Pass	5♡	Pass	6♠
End			

The Headmaster led ♣J and down went the dummy. 'Only 15 points?' queried the Matron. 'I thought you'd have more than that for a jump-raise. Small, please.'

Matron won the first trick with the club king, cashed ♡A, and ruffed a heart. She then ran the jack of trumps, pleased to see this win the trick. The trump ten brought less good news – East showing out. The Headmaster won with the king and was quick to return ♡K, forcing the dummy's last trump.

Oh dear, thought the Matron. How had that happened? She was stuck in dummy and seemed to have no way to reach her hand, to draw the last trump. There was no alternative but to play the top diamonds. The Headmaster ruffed the third round and the Matron was now two down, since she had to lose a club as well.

'Yes, I only made game,' said the Matron. 'A raise to Two Spades would be quite enough on your hand, Molly.'

The Headmaster smiled at his partner. 'You liked my duck of the trump king?' he said. 'I thought it might draw dividends.'

'The slam was cold,' Madame Baguette replied. 'Win the club lead in dummy and play on trumps. What could be easier?'

A round or two later, facing Stuart Melchett and Julian Dyer, the Headmaster was first to speak on this deal:

North–South game
Dealer West

♠ A 10 9 5
♡ K 9 7
♢ A Q 6 3
♣ A 3

♠ 6
♡ 10 8 5
♢ 10 4
♣ K Q J 8 6 5 4

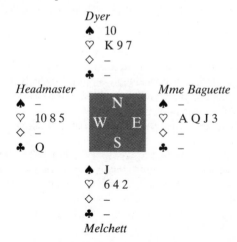

♠ 8 4 2
♡ A Q J 3
♢ J 9 8 5
♣ 9 7

♠ K Q J 7 3
♡ 6 4 2
♢ K 7 2
♣ 10 2

WEST	NORTH	EAST	SOUTH
Head-	Julian	Madame	Stuart
master	Dyer	Baguette	Melchett
3♣	Dble	Pass	4♠
End			

The king of clubs was led and Stuart Melchett peered at the dummy through his horn-rimmed spectacles. 'Ace, please,' he said.

Trumps were drawn in three rounds and declarer then tested the diamonds, West showing out on the third round. Madame Baguette won the fourth round of diamonds and Melchett threw his last club, leaving the safe hand on lead. He ruffed East's club exit in his hand and surveyed this end position:

Dyer
♠ 10
♡ K 9 7
♢ –
♣ –

Headmaster
♠ –
♡ 10 8 5
♢ –
♣ Q

Mme Baguette
♠ –
♡ A Q J 3
♢ –
♣ –

♠ J
♡ 6 4 2
♢ –
♣ –
Melchett

The young declarer did not like the look of it. The ace of hearts was marked offside by the bidding and, unless the Headmaster was asleep, he would surely insert a card high enough to force dummy's king.

Melchett was about to lead a heart, hoping for the best, when an intriguing idea occurred to him. What if he cashed the trump winner first? If Madame Baguette held ♡A Q J x, she might well throw her low heart and would then have to win the first heart trick!

When Melchett led the jack of trumps, the Headmaster threw his last club. Madame Baguette lost no time in throwing her ♡3. At least the Headmaster would be happy with her on this hand, she thought. With her A Q J sitting over dummy's king, the last three tricks would surely be hers.

Melchett now led a heart, covering West's 5 with the dummy's 7. Madame Baguette looked as if she had been stabbed in the back. *Incroyable*! One of her certain tricks had vanished into the air. She won with the jack and then had to concede a trick to dummy's ♡K. The game had been made.

'That wasn't very clever!' exclaimed the Headmaster. 'You were bound to be end-played if you held on to your three top hearts.'

Madame Baguette looked back uncertainly. She should have thrown an honour away? Is that what he was saying?

'You must throw the queen of hearts and keep ace-jack and another,' continued the Headmaster loudly. 'Then I can put in the 10 to stop the end-play.'

'Does that work, Headmaster?' asked Julian Dyer. 'I cover with the king and dummy's 9 would make a trick.'

The Headmaster's eyes bulged and his face deepened by several shades of red. 'If I require any assistance in my analysis, I will ask for it!' he cried.

Julian Dyer froze in his seat, not daring to move a muscle.

'The word "humility" is obviously not in your vocabulary,' shouted the Headmaster. 'Do you think great men like General Eisenhower go around, bragging like that – telling everyone how clever they are?'

Play had stopped at the adjoining tables and several pairs of eyes were focussed on the table.

'No, Sir,' said Dyer, eventually daring to speak. 'I'm sorry, Sir. How shall I score the board?'

'What on earth does the score matter?' said the Headmaster. 'If we have no manners in this world, we are as nothing.' He assumed his blackest expression and flexed his right arm briefly. 'You will report to my study, after prayers tomorrow morning.'

Madame Baguette had been about to point out that the Headmaster could have beaten the contract by leading a heart. Perhaps now was not the best moment, she decided.

A few rounds later, Phillip Glasson and Yvonne Goutier arrived at the table. The Headmaster averted his eyes as the scantily-clad French girl took her seat. Rumour had it that Glasson was quite smitten with the girl. No wonder!

The Headmaster summoned his concentration. He had better set a competent impression, facing two relatively new members of the staff.

```
Love All              ♠ K 2
Dealer South          ♡ A K J 8 7 3
                      ◇ 6 4
                      ♣ 6 4 2

      ♠ J 10 9 7        N          ♠ Q 8 5
      ♡ 2          W        E      ♡ 10 9 4
      ◇ K J 8 5 3                  ◇ 10 9 7 2
      ♣ 10 8 5          S          ♣ Q 9 7

                      ♠ A 6 4 3
                      ♡ Q 6 5
                      ◇ A Q
                      ♣ A K J 3
```

WEST	NORTH	EAST	SOUTH
Phillip	Madame	Mlle	Head-
Glasson	Baguette	Goutier	master
–	–	–	2NT
Pass	3◇	Pass	3♡
Pass	6♡	End	

A transfer sequence carried the Headmaster to Six Hearts and Phillip Glasson led ♠J. 'Thank you, er . . . Bernice,' said the Headmaster, as the dummy appeared.

He paused to consider his line of play. The contract was at risk only if West held both the missing minor-suit cards. What could be done in that case? Ah yes, there was an interesting extra-chance play, involving the spade suit. Thank heavens he was at the helm and not the Baguette woman. 'Play the king, please,' he said.

The Headmaster drew trumps in three rounds, then cashed the ace of spades and ruffed a spade. A club to the ace left these cards to be played:

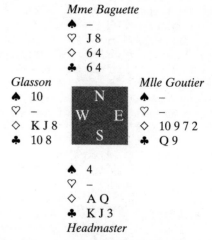

Mme Baguette
♠ –
♡ J 8
♦ 6 4
♣ 6 4

Glasson
♠ 10
♡ –
♦ K J 8
♣ 10 8

Mlle Goutier
♠ –
♡ –
♦ 10 9 7 2
♣ Q 9

♠ 4
♡ –
♦ A Q
♣ K J 3
Headmaster

The Headmaster led his last spade, covered by West's 10, Madame Baguette's heavily jewelled fingers reached for a trump. 'No, no!' exclaimed the Headmaster. 'Throw a club, please.'

The Headmaster turned triumphantly towards Glasson, facing his cards. 'You must lead into one of my minor-suit tenaces,' he informed him. 'It's twelve tricks, whatever you do.'

'You played it well, Headmaster,' said Phillip Glasson.

The Headmaster nodded. Had Madame Baguette been the declarer, she would have ruffed the fourth spade and relied on some luck in the minors. It was not his way to depend on finesses. A top-class player could usually find some way to avoid them.

'It's a bottom,' Madame Baguette announced, inspecting the score-sheet. 'Everyone else has an overtrick. There was no need to lose that spade trick.'

The Headmaster reached for Yvonne Goutier's curtain card. Just his luck! Clubs 3-3 with the queen onside. 'I can't help it if the whole room misplays the hand,' he declared. 'A loser-on-loser play like that would have graced a Bermuda Bowl final.'

'Quite possibly,' Madame Baguette replied. 'The Bermuda Bowl is not a pairs event, of course.'

The next hour or so passed by without special incident. The last round then saw the arrival at the Headmaster's table of Peter

Cummings and Norris Butcher. The Headmaster was first to speak on this deal:

North–South game
Dealer South

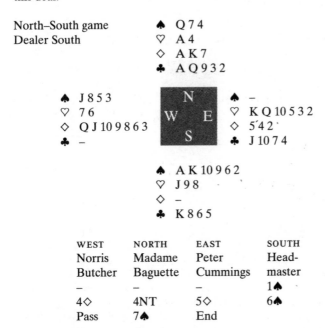

	♠	Q 7 4
	♡	A 4
	◇	A K 7
	♣	A Q 9 3 2

♠ J 8 5 3
♡ 7 6
◇ Q J 10 9 8 6 3
♣ —

♠ —
♡ K Q 10 5 3 2
◇ 5 4 2
♣ J 10 7 4

♠ A K 10 9 6 2
♡ J 9 8
◇ —
♣ K 8 6 5

WEST	NORTH	EAST	SOUTH
Norris	Madame	Peter	Head-
Butcher	Baguette	Cummings	master
–	–	–	1♠
4◇	4NT	5◇	6♠
Pass	7♠	End	

Hoping that his bold pre-emption had pushed the opponents too high, Norris Butcher led ◇Q.

'Such a hand I have for you,' declared Madame Baguette, as she laid out the dummy.

The Headmaster nodded approvingly. Yes, if both black suits behaved there were fourteen tricks on top. It would be an excellent board for them. A successful grand always scored 90% or so in this field.

The Headmaster won the diamond lead with the ace, throwing a heart from his hand. When he cashed the ace of trumps East showed out. I don't mind that, thought the Headmaster, leading ♠10 from his hand. Norris Butcher declined to cover and the 10 won the trick. A trump to the queen was followed by a diamond ruff and the king of trumps.

Before playing on clubs, the Headmaster decided to cash his remaining trumps. Even if it made no difference, it would still look impressive. This was the position after all the trumps had been played:

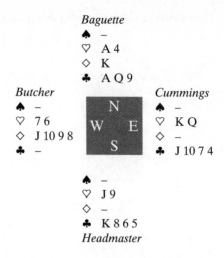

Baguette
♠ –
♡ A 4
♢ K
♣ A Q 9

Butcher
♠ –
♡ 7 6
♢ J 10 9 8
♣ –

Cummings
♠ –
♡ K Q
♢ –
♣ J 10 7 4

♠ –
♡ J 9
♢ –
♣ K 8 6 5
Headmaster

The Headmaster led a club towards dummy and could not believe it when West showed out on the first round. There was no justice in the world! They bid a superb grand slam, despite a pre-emptive barrage from the opponents, then both the black suits break 4-0. 'Ace, please,' he said.

The Headmaster cashed ♡A, dropping the queen from East. When he continued with the king of diamonds, he noted with approval that Cummings was squirming in his seat. Excellent! If he held the other heart honour, he would have no good discard.

Cummings eventually discarded ♡K, hoping that his partner held the jack. The Headmaster discarded a club and triumphantly faced his remaining cards. 'Grand slam bid and made!' he announced in a voice that could be heard across the room. 'I caught you in a squeeze there, Peter.'

'Best to keep your voice down, Headmaster,' Cummings replied. 'There may be others still to play it.'

'Don't be silly, it's the last round,' said the Headmaster. 'In any case, I don't think anyone else in the room is capable of landing thirteen tricks against breaks like that.'

Madame Baguette inspected the score-sheet happily. 'Well done, Headmaster,' she exclaimed. 'It's a nice top for us.'

'It doesn't surprise me,' the Headmaster replied. He directed a warm smile towards Madame Baguette. 'You won't have seen card-play like that, partnering the Matron!'

13. The Headmaster's Forgotten Lesson

A crowd of boys had gathered round the bridge notice board, where this announcement had just been posted:

> *The following teams will contest the annual*
>   *Masters v Boys match:*
>
>   *Masters: A.J.F. Doulton (capt), Reverend Benson*
>   *B.T. Bellis, P.C. Cutforth*
>
>   *Boys: Stephen Sutcliffe (capt), James Dakin*
>   *John Hutson, Neil Phillips*
>
> *The match will take place in the Dyne Library at 7p.m.*
> *on Friday 21st July. Well-behaved spectators are welcome.*
>   *AJFD*

'Should be a laugh,' a member of the third form observed. 'I'm going to get there ten minutes early, to get a good view.'

The match started punctually and this was an early hand:

East–West game
Dealer South

	♠ A K
	♡ A K 10 7 6
	◇ Q 3
	♣ A 10 7 5

	N	
♠ Q 7 6 4	W E	♠ J 8 2
♡ 9 3		♡ Q J 8 5 2
◇ K J 6	S	◇ 7 2
♣ K Q J 2		♣ 9 6 4

	♠ 10 9 5 3
	♡ 4
	◇ A 10 9 8 5 4
	♣ 8 3

WEST	NORTH	EAST	SOUTH
Head-	Neil	Reverend	John
master	Phillips	Benson	Hutson
–	–	–	3◇
Pass	6◇	End	

116

The Headmaster saw no reason to double the diamond slam. If the boys had bid to some absurd contract, a big swing would come his way with or without a double. He led ♣K and down went the dummy. The red-haired John Hutson surveyed it with no great approval. 'It was a non-vulnerable pre-empt, Neil,' he said.

That's what I like to hear, thought the Headmaster. If the boys lost a packet on the first board they would doubtless try to get it straight back on the second board. The Masters would then be 20 IMPs ahead before the match had really got going.

Hutson won the club lead with the ace and played two rounds of hearts, throwing his club loser. What now? The only hope was to crossruff and hope for some miracle in the end position. 'Ace of spades, please,' he said.

Hutson cashed both of dummy's spade honours, then ruffed a club in the South hand. A spade ruff with the 3 was followed by a second club ruff. When Hutson ruffed his last spade with the queen, East was unable to overruff. This position had been reached:

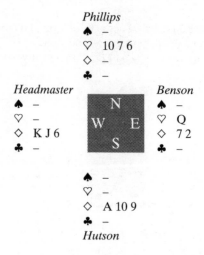

Phillips
♠ –
♡ 10 7 6
♢ –
♣ –

Headmaster
♠ –
♡ –
♢ K J 6
♣ –

Benson
♠ –
♡ Q
♢ 7 2
♣ –

Hutson
♠ –
♡ –
♢ A 10 9
♣ –

Hutson's heart was beating faster by the moment. He was going to make this contract! He led a heart from dummy and ruffed with the 9. The Headmaster overruffed with the jack but had to lead back into declarer's trump tenace. Twelve tricks had been made.

Prolonged applause broke out from the onlookers. 'Well done, Johnny!' someone called out.

The Headmaster spun round. 'Be quiet!' he cried. 'This isn't a Varsity rugby match. If you can't behave appropriately, I will have the room cleared.'

Silence reigned as the Headmaster made the unwelcome insertion on his score-card. 'Absurd opening bid, of course,' he informed the Reverend Benson. 'I don't expect Bertie and Percy will reach the slam.'

The Reverend Benson smiled to himself. '*Caveat preemptor*, Headmaster,' he said.

At the other table, Bertie Bellis was occupying his favourite South seat. He sorted his cards for the next deal, then held them above his head for the benefit of the onlookers behind him.

Game All
Dealer East

	♠ A Q 5 2	
	♡ 7 5	
	◇ Q J 8 2	
	♣ A 7 3	

♠ 9 4		♠ K J 8 7 6 3
♡ K J 9 6 3	N	♡ 4
◇ 7 5	W E	◇ 10 4
♣ 10 8 6 5	S	♣ Q J 9 2

	♠ 10	
	♡ A Q 10 8 2	
	◇ A K 9 6 3	
	♣ K 4	

WEST	NORTH	EAST	SOUTH
James	Percy	Stephen	Bertie
Dakin	Cutforth	Sutcliffe	Bellis
–	–	2♠	3♡
Pass	3♠	Pass	4◇
Pass	4NT	Pass	5♡
Pass	6◇	End	

The boys' captain, Stephen Sutcliffe, opened with a Weak Two in spades. Bertie Bellis was soon in Six Diamonds and West led ♠9.

Bellis won with dummy's ♠A and drew trumps in two rounds. He then addressed his mind to the heart suit. If hearts broke 4-2, he could afford to give up a heart, if necessary, and ruff the suit good. What if West held five hearts, though? Bellis soon spotted the answer. 'Seven of hearts, please,' he said.

When East followed with the 4, Bellis allowed dummy's 7 to run. Dakin won with the 9 and the contract was now secure. East showed out on ♡A but a double ruffing finesse against the king and jack brought home the contract.

Sutcliffe turned admiringly towards Bellis, a hero of his. 'You go down if you play a heart to the 10 or queen, don't you?' he said.

Bellis nodded. 'I think so,' he replied. 'I'd have to play the ace next, then James could cover each of my remaining hearts.'

It was one of the Maths master's endearing qualities that once boys had reached the fifth form he addressed them by their first names. No other master would consider it.

Back on the Headmaster's table, the players drew their cards for this deal:

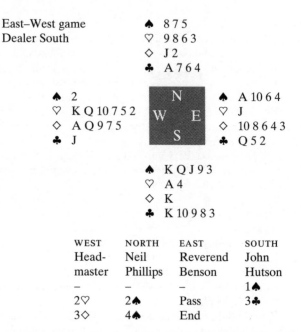

```
East–West game        ♠ 8 7 5
Dealer South          ♡ 9 8 6 3
                      ◇ J 2
                      ♣ A 7 6 4

      ♠ 2                           ♠ A 10 6 4
      ♡ K Q 10 7 5 2        N       ♡ J
      ◇ A Q 9 7 5       W       E   ◇ 10 8 6 4 3
      ♣ J                   S       ♣ Q 5 2

                      ♠ K Q J 9 3
                      ♡ A 4
                      ◇ K
                      ♣ K 10 9 8 3
```

WEST	NORTH	EAST	SOUTH
Head-	Neil	Reverend	John
master	Phillips	Benson	Hutson
–	–	–	1♠
2♡	2♠	Pass	3♣
3◇	4♠	End	

The Headmaster led ♡K against Four Spades and down went the dummy. 'How on earth can you accept the game-try on that hand?' he demanded. 'Only three trumps and ten losers? Did you attend my lecture on the Losing Trick Count?'

'Yes, but I thought my club holding might be useful,' replied Neil Phillips.

'Many of the world's most foolish statements have begun with the words: Yes, but . . .' declared the Headmaster. 'You youngsters think you know so much. If only you'd listen to those with more experience, your game would improve no end.'

John Hutson captured the heart lead with the ace and played the king of trumps. Benson won immediately and switched to a low diamond, drawing the king and ace. The Headmaster cashed the queen of hearts and continued with the other red queen, declarer ruffing. When Hutson played a second top trump the Headmaster showed out. What now?

Hutson attempted to count the hand. Charlie B had returned ♢4 and played ♢3 on the next round. It therefore seemed that the diamonds were 5-5. The Headmaster must have 1-6-5-1 shape and his club singleton would have to be an honour to allow the suit to be picked up. How could he take a club finesse and a spade finesse, when the ♣A was the only entry to dummy?

Sutcliffe eventually saw how it could be done. He led ♣10 from his hand, covered by the jack and ace. 'Seven of clubs, please,' he said.

Had Benson covered this card, declarer would have returned to dummy with ♣6 to take the marked finesse in trumps. Benson in fact played low and – thanks to declarer's unblock of the ten – the seven could be run successfully. Still in dummy, the young declarer called for a trump and took the marked finesse of the nine. A few seconds later he had ten tricks before him.

The Headmaster glared across the table. 'Five-card diamond support, Charles?' he cried. 'Why in the name of Heaven didn't you bid Five Diamonds?'

The spectators within the Headmaster's range of vision fought desperately to maintain a straight face. Superb! This was the sort of exchange they had come to watch.

'I don't believe in sacrificing at adverse vulnerability,' Benson replied. 'The policy has served me well over the years.'

'What do you mean, sacrificing?' persisted the Headmaster. 'Five Diamonds was absolutely frigid! We could lose a double game swing on the board.'

'You may be right on this occasion,' said Benson, 'but a wild bid at the five-level would hardly set a good example to these boys watching.' He gazed fondly at the young kibitzers surrounding the table. 'The boys are always my prime concern, Headmaster,' he said. 'If I caused them to pick up any bad habits at the five-level, I would never forgive myself.'

Back on the other table, Bertie Bellis was occupying the hot seat once again.

East–West game
Dealer East

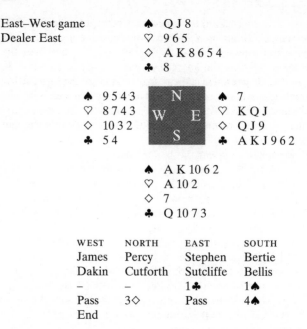

```
                      ♠ Q J 8
                      ♡ 9 6 5
                      ◇ A K 8 6 5 4
                      ♣ 8
    ♠ 9 5 4 3                        ♠ 7
    ♡ 8 7 4 3          N             ♡ K Q J
    ◇ 10 3 2        W     E          ◇ Q J 9
    ♣ 5 4              S             ♣ A K J 9 6 2
                      ♠ A K 10 6 2
                      ♡ A 10 2
                      ◇ 7
                      ♣ Q 10 7 3
```

WEST	NORTH	EAST	SOUTH
James	Percy	Stephen	Bertie
Dakin	Cutforth	Sutcliffe	Bellis
–	–	1♣	1♠
Pass	3◇	Pass	4♠
End			

'You alerted the 3◇?' queried James Dakin, who was on lead.

'A small invention of mine,' Bertie Bellis replied. 'We call it a fit-jump. It shows spade support and a good side suit in diamonds.'

Sutcliffe won the club lead with the king and returned ♡K, taken by declarer's ace. Bertie Bellis drew one round of trumps with the ace, then cashed the two top diamonds in dummy, throwing one of his heart losers. His next move was to ruff a diamond high, the suit proving to be 3-3.

A trump to the queen brought less good news, a 4-1 break, but Bellis could see a way round this. 'Diamond, please,' he said. He threw his last heart and West ruffed with his penultimate trump.

James Dakin tried his luck with another round of clubs, but Bellis countered by throwing a heart from the dummy. East won with the club king and this was the defenders' last trick. Dummy's jack of trumps would serve as an entry to the remaining diamonds.

Due mainly to a fine card from Bellis and Cutforth, the Masters led by 32 IMPs to 25 at the interval. The traditional refreshments for the match consisted of two fruit cakes, baked by Grace Doulton, the Headmaster's wife.

'For Heaven's sake, Hutson!' exclaimed the Headmaster, spotting the fourth-former dunking a slice of cake into his Coca-Cola. 'Where are your manners?'

'Sorry, Sir,' Hutson replied. 'It tastes miles better like that.'

'Your parents are not paying nine-hundred pounds a year to have you devour your food like a savage in the jungle,' continued the Headmaster.

Reverend Benson peered disapprovingly over his rimless spectacles. 'I don't think that's a very enlightened metaphor, Headmaster,' he observed. 'The cake is a bit dry, actually.'

The match restarted with the two captains in opposition. The first big contract fell to Stephen Sutcliffe:

```
Love All                    ♠ A K J 4 2
Dealer South                ♡ 8 7 4
                            ◇ Q J 7
                            ♣ A K

         ♠ 8 6              N            ♠ 9 7
         ♡ K 9 3       W         E       ♡ J 10 6 5 2
         ◇ K 10 5 4                      ◇ 8 6
         ♣ J 10 9 2         S            ♣ 8 7 6 4

                            ♠ Q 10 5 3
                            ♡ A Q
                            ◇ A 9 3 2
                            ♣ Q 5 3
```

WEST	NORTH	EAST	SOUTH
Head-	James	Reverend	Stephen
master	Dakin	Benson	Sutcliffe
–	–	–	1NT
Pass	2♡	Pass	3♠
Pass	6♠	End	

Sutcliffe decided to break the transfer response, despite the unproductive six points in his doubleton heart holding. Dakin went straight to a small slam and the Headmaster led ♣J.

Sutcliffe surveyed the dummy thoughtfully. How should he tackle the red suits? If he played a diamond towards the queen and East won with the king, a heart return would be awkward. He would have to decide whether to finesse before he knew if the diamond suit would yield three tricks, giving him a second heart discard from dummy.

A better plan occurred to the young declarer. He won the club lead with the ace and cashed dummy's other high club. After a trump to the queen, he cashed ♣Q, throwing a heart from dummy. A trump to the ace drew the outstanding trumps. 'Queen of diamonds, please,' said Sutcliffe.

The ◇8 appeared from East and declarer followed with ◇2. The Headmaster did not like the look of this at all. Benson's ◇8 apparently proclaimed a doubleton, leaving South with four diamonds to the A 9. If he won with the diamond king he might well be endplayed. Hoping for salvation from some quarter, the Headmaster allowed the diamond queen to win. 'Jack of diamonds, please,' said Sutcliffe, proceeding to run the card.

The Headmaster, who could delay the issue no longer, won with the king. The diamond situation was known, so his only chance was a heart, in the hope that East held the queen. Benson could produce only the jack of hearts and declarer claimed the remainder. The slam had been made.

'Well done,' congratulated James Dakin.

'A diamond towards the queen-jack would have worked too,' Sutcliffe replied. 'No reason to expect a swing.'

At the other table Bertie Bellis was preserving his reputation for picking up good hands:

North–South game
Dealer West

```
                    ♠  A K J 4
                    ♡  5 4
                    ◇  6 4 3
                    ♣  8 4 3 2

    ♠  8                              ♠  Q 10 9 7 6 3
    ♡  J 10 9 7 6 3 2       N         ♡  8
    ◇  9                W      E      ◇  10 8 7 5 2
    ♣  Q J 10 7            S          ♣  9

                    ♠  5 2
                    ♡  A K Q
                    ◇  A K Q J
                    ♣  A K 6 5
```

WEST	NORTH	EAST	SOUTH
John	Percy	Neil	Bertie
Hutson	Cutforth	Phillips	Bellis
3♡	Pass	Pass	Dble
Pass	3♠	Pass	3NT
Pass	4NT	Pass	6NT
End			

Realising that his partner was showing a hand too strong for an initial 3NT overcall, Percy Cutforth suggested a slam by raising to 4NT. Bertie Bellis was happy to accept the invitation. He won the ♣Q lead with the ace and cashed ♣K, East discarding a spade. Two rounds of diamonds, West showing out on the second round, gave him a complete count on the hand. Yes, he could surely make the slam by end-playing East in spades.

Declarer's next move was to cash three rounds of hearts. East could not afford to reduce to three spades, or declarer would simply play a spade to the jack, setting up a long spade in dummy. He therefore had to throw his fifth diamond. Bertie Bellis now cashed his remaining two diamonds, leaving this end position:

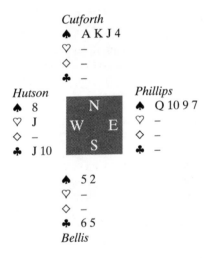

Cutforth
♠ A K J 4
♡ –
♢ –
♣ –

Hutson
♠ 8
♡ J
♢ –
♣ J 10

Phillips
♠ Q 10 9 7
♡ –
♢ –
♣ –

Bellis
♠ 5 2
♡ –
♢ –
♣ 6 5

Bertie Bellis crossed to the ace of spades. 'Small spade, please,' he said.

Neil Phillips nodded in admiration, facing his remaining cards by way of conceding the contract. 'Wow!' he said. 'There was nothing I could do. If I throw a spade instead of the long diamond, he can set up the spade suit.'

Bertie Bellis's eyes were alight. 'Exactly the same end-play was possible on your partner too,' he observed. 'When your ♣9 fell at trick one, I could have cashed two spades followed by four rounds of diamonds. Hutson would have to throw four hearts to keep all his clubs, to prevent me ducking a club.'

'I see!' said Neil Phillips. 'You could then draw his hearts and lead a club towards the 8 to end-play him.'

124

'That's it,' replied the Maths master. 'Rather an elegant symmetry, don't you think?'

Few of the onlookers could follow the discussion. As far as they were concerned, Bertie might have been explaining some theorem in Differential Topology.

Back at the Headmaster's table, Stephen Sutcliffe had arrived in another taxing contract.

Love All
Dealer South

♠ 7 5
♡ K 10 8 7 3
◇ A 10 6 3
♣ J 8

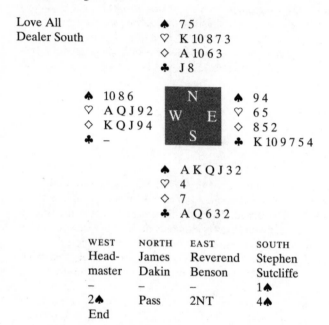

♠ 10 8 6
♡ A Q J 9 2
◇ K Q J 9 4
♣ —

♠ 9 4
♡ 6 5
◇ 8 5 2
♣ K 10 9 7 5 4

♠ A K Q J 3 2
♡ 4
◇ 7
♣ A Q 6 3 2

WEST	NORTH	EAST	SOUTH
Head-	James	Reverend	Stephen
master	Dakin	Benson	Sutcliffe
–	–	–	1♠
2♠	Pass	2NT	4♠
End			

The Headmaster's Michaels cue-bid showed hearts and a minor. Benson's 2NT asked which minor his partner held and Sutcliffe closed the auction with a jump to 4♠.

Sutcliffe won the king of diamonds lead in the dummy and drew trumps, noting that Headmaster held three cards in the suit. Since he had led a diamond at Trick 1, the Michaels cue-bid marked his shape as 3-5-5-0.

At Trick 5 Sutcliffe led a heart from his hand. The Headmaster rose with the ace and now had to play one or other red suit. A heart to dummy's king would allow declarer to score six trumps, one heart, one diamond and two clubs. Unwilling to give the lead to dummy, the Headmaster tried the effect of playing the diamond queen. Sutcliffe allowed this card to win, throwing a club from his hand.

These cards remained:

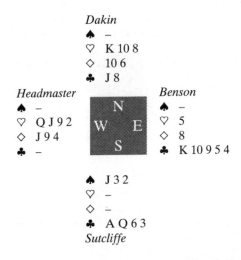

Dakin
♠ –
♡ K 10 8
♢ 10 6
♣ J 8

Headmaster
♠ –
♡ Q J 9 2
♢ J 9 4
♣ –

Benson
♠ –
♡ 5
♢ 8
♣ K 10 9 5 4

♠ J 3 2
♡ –
♢ –
♣ A Q 6 3
Sutcliffe

The Headmaster continued with ♢J but Sutcliffe allowed this card to win too, throwing another club. It was the end of the line, as far as the defence was concerned. The Headmaster had to give the lead to dummy and declarer could now claim the contract. He threw two more clubs from his hand, not even needing to take the club finesse.

The Headmaster returned his cards to the wallet somewhat ungraciously. 'Very lucky to find me with no clubs,' he muttered.

'I think I was safe however many clubs you held,' Sutcliffe replied. 'If you turned up with two trumps and one club, I could cash the ace of clubs before playing a heart. If you had one trump and two clubs, I could simply set up the clubs, losing two clubs and a heart.'

Benson nodded his agreement. 'Your Michaels bid was rather helpful to him, Headmaster,' he observed. 'If you don't bid, declarer might try a club finesse at Trick 2. He goes down, then.'

'A somewhat pointless observation, seeing that I held a five-loser hand and two good suits,' declared the Headmaster. 'The boys misjudged the auction, anyway. 3NT is an easy make.'

A hand or two later Sutcliffe arrived in a slam:

Game All   ♠ 5 3 2
Dealer South   ♡ 8 6 3
               ♢ 10 5 2
               ♣ K J 10 9

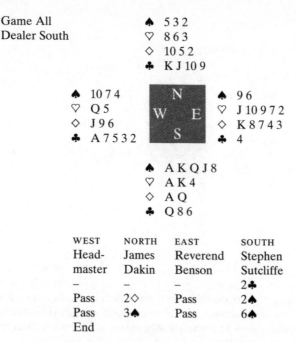

	♠ 10 7 4		♠ 9 6
	♡ Q 5		♡ J 10 9 7 2
	♢ J 9 6		♢ K 8 7 4 3
	♣ A 7 5 3 2		♣ 4

               ♠ A K Q J 8
               ♡ A K 4
               ♢ A Q
               ♣ Q 8 6

WEST	NORTH	EAST	SOUTH
Head-	James	Reverend	Stephen
master	Dakin	Benson	Sutcliffe
–	–	–	2♣
Pass	2♢	Pass	2♠
Pass	3♠	Pass	6♠
End			

The Headmaster led a trump and down went the dummy. 'Is that all?' queried Sutcliffe. 'I thought Three Spades showed good values, like a single raise of an Acol Two.'

'We don't have all night,' declared the Headmaster. 'If you've messed up this one, get it over with quickly and we can move on to the next board.'

Sutcliffe drew trumps in three rounds and played ♣6, drawing the two, nine and four. Taking advantage of the entry to dummy, he finessed the queen of diamonds. When this manoeuvre proved successful, he cashed the diamond ace and led another club from his hand.

The Headmaster paused to consider his defence. Benson had played the four on the first round of clubs. Since this was the lowest spot-card out, he could not have started with a doubleton in the suit. Declarer was marked with three clubs and the ace would have to be held up again.

Dummy's ten won the second round of clubs and the young declarer then ruffed a diamond. These cards remained:

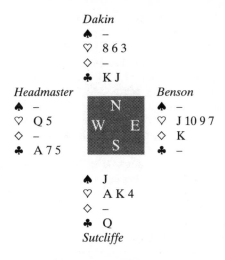

Dakin
♠ —
♡ 8 6 3
◇ —
♣ K J

Headmaster
♠ —
♡ Q 5
◇ —
♣ A 7 5

Benson
♠ —
♡ J 10 9 7
◇ K
♣ —

♠ J
♡ A K 4
◇ —
♣ Q
Sutcliffe

Sutcliffe surveyed the scene exultantly. Captain of the team, and with so many boys watching, he was about to endplay the Headmaster! It wasn't just some wonderful dream, was it? He cashed the two top hearts, then exited with ♣Q. The Headmaster won with the ace and had to concede a trick to dummy's ♣K. Away went declarer's heart loser and the slam had been made.

The Reverend Benson looked as if the end of the world had arrived. 'I had a singleton club, Headmaster!' he cried. 'Lead the ace of clubs and I get a ruff.'

'Don't be absurd,' snapped the Headmaster. 'Whoever heard of leading an ace when the strong hand is on your right?'

It was too much for the cleric to endure. 'Of course you must lead an ace against a slam,' he declared. 'Don't you remember those two slams you let through against Spencer Grove?'

The young spectators' eyes were alight. What a splendid evening's entertainment it had been.

Only one thing could make it perfect. A result in the right direction. The match drew to a close and a tense final comparison, confirmed by several further checks, did indeed reveal that the boys had won by 2 IMPs.

The Headmaster tore his score-card in two and tossed it into a nearby wastepaper basket. 'The Staff have never lost to the Boys before, not in twenty years,' he declared. He puffed furiously at his pipe, then turned towards the Maths master. 'You're losing your touch, Bertie.'

Bertie Bellis glanced at the well-stocked plus column of his score-card. 'Yes, I think we might have beaten that 3♢ contract on Board 22,' he replied. 'Suppose I lead a trump, Percy. When you take your ace of clubs, you can play another trump and . . .'

'I'm not talking about part-scores!' thundered the Headmaster. 'What about all these double-figure swings we lost?'

Bertie Bellis was finding it hard to keep a straight face. 'I think you should welcome this defeat, Headmaster,' he said. 'It's a remarkable demonstration of how well the boys have flourished under your instruction.'

'I polished the trophy last night, Headmaster,' said the Reverend Benson. He placed the gleaming cup on the table and proceeded to inspect the engravings on the plinth. 'You were quite right about the previous results. It says Masters, Masters, Masters, Masters . . . all the way back to 1944.'

The Headmaster strode towards the doorway, a stream of smoke following in his wake. 'You may present the trophy, Charles,' he said. 'I've wasted enough time this evening!'